A WORLD OI

A REDEMPTIVE

Solly Kaplinski

"Do you not see how necessary a world of pains and troubles
is to school intelligence and make it a soul?"
John Keats

"A path leads to Ponar
There is no way to return."

S'firn vegn tsu Ponar tsu,
S'firt keyn veg tsurik,
Shmerke Kaczerginski (1908 – 1954)

"The heart has not revealed it to the mouth."
Kohelet Rabbah – a commentary on Ecclesiastes

First published 2015

To the Kaplinsky family
May 2016
Let's stay in touch
with love,
Solly

CONTENTS

A World of Pains, Solly Kaplinski, 2015

Dedication

Dedicated with love to:

My *Bobbas* and *Zeidas* whom I never knew

My parents of blessed memory whom I knew too briefly

My wife Arleen and children: Tali, Ronit and Carmi

Who know me so well

And to the heroic Tuvia and Asael Bielski who gave Sima and Itzel – and us, life and freedom

Author's Introduction

If I have to try to guess when the seeds for this story started to germinate, I would turn the clock back to September 4, 2003.

On that day, Israeli pilots flew three F -15 jets over the Auschwitz – Birkenau extermination camp.

At the same time, the names of victims of the transport from Drancy, France that arrived 60 years earlier at Auschwitz on September 4, 1943 and who were sent to their death in the gas chambers a few hours after their arrival, were read out at a ceremony on the ground at Auschwitz.

Fast forward two years later to the opening of the new Yad Vashem Museum – Israel's living memorial to the Holocaust.

At one of the events to honor the occasion, the chief pilot who flew over Auschwitz together with five other crewmembers whose relatives were survivors of the Holocaust, recounted his very moving story to an overflowing lecture theatre of several hundred guests at an aircraft base.

A World of Pains, Solly Kaplinski, 2015

During the flight, General Avi Maor read the following sentence to his companions, which has become a symbol of the entire flyover: "We, Israeli Air Force pilots, in the skies above this camp of horrors, rose from the ashes of millions of victims. We carry their silent cries, salute their heroism and promise to be a shield for the Jewish people and their country, Israel."

He was quoted later as saying:

"From the moment of take-off it was all very technical, like every flight. Only a year later, after we all met up, did we discover that we all experienced the same phenomenon as soon as we moved over Auschwitz. We were in tandem aircrafts, and usually we talk a lot during the flight. The same second, we all fell silent. A silence so loud, as if something heavy had fallen on the air and we all understood exactly the magnitude of what we were doing."

During the Q and A after the pilot's presentation, one of the people in the audience came up to the platform where the pilot was standing. To a hushed audience he said the following:

"In Isaiah Chapter 60 verse 14 it reads:

'The sons of the oppressors, those who afflicted you, will come and bow down before you and kiss your feet.'

I am the son of a German officer who served in army artillery combat unit.

I was a soldier of the German air force. Therefore, I come to you and I bow down."

There wasn't a dry eye in the room as he knelt down at the pilot's feet and asked for forgiveness.

As a witness to this very emotional event, it occurred to me when I was able to regain my balance, that it is somehow more palatable while still being traumatic for the second generation, children of Nazis, to try to make amends.

Their parents, the actual perpetrators were either unwilling or unable to confront their past – or were in total denial.

As someone who grew up in the long shadow of the Holocaust, I often wondered why so many years after the Shoah, there were very few, if any, murderers who expressed feelings of guilt or sorrow for the crimes they committed.

They may have in the interim become successful politicians, learned judges, accomplished lawyers, outstanding doctors, wealthy industrialists, respected school principals or dignified ministers of the church but never a word of regret or remorse, no acknowledgement.

A World of Pains, Solly Kaplinski, 2015

Many of those who were put on trial after the war claimed that they were 'following orders', that they were just a cog in the machine or expressed regrets that they "didn't finish the job."

There is a universality of not taking personal responsibility for crimes committed during wartime - both on the personal level as well as on the country level and of course our prisons are full of innocent people!

Through the lens of Jonathan Varnas, a very successful, highly accomplished and prize - winning human rights lawyer in the US who focuses especially on supporting vulnerable children, this novella explores the theme of accountability for long forgotten and repressed savage crimes more than fifty years after they were committed.

It also focuses on how the perpetrator deals with 'newly discovered' realities of his horrifying situation, the choices he makes in terms of publically exposing the bitter truth and a possible measure of redemption accomplished through his final shocking deed.

This is also a story about remembrance of and paying homage to family members unknown and their brutal fate in the killing fields of Vilnius.

According to Arleen, my wife, who sometimes doubles up as my therapist – more often than not (!), my struggle with this creative process over a long period of time, is in reality a very personal and cathartic story about mourning for my family - and the fact that no one expressed remorse nor apologized to me for the misfortune and tragedy that befell members of my family who perished in the Shoah. Those who committed these crimes against my family – and against me, did not get the justice they deserved.

In this respect, this "case study" is, in the final analysis, also about the impact of the Shoah on the second generation: children of Holocaust survivors and the burdens - and blessings they shoulder - faced with the responsibility as survivors pass on, of carrying this heavy torch and being the messengers for the next generation.

Solly Kaplinski

Jerusalem, Rosh Hashanah, 2015

kapfam@netvision.net.il

Prologue

AN ORPHAN'S LAMENT - LEGACY ON MY SHOULDER
(The burden of history)

I owe it to you Mom and Dad
even though you rest in the earth
to go home

I owe it to you my Bobba and Zeida*
whom I never knew
whose warm embrace and loving caress I could only imagine
and who were geshiesen **
and geshaysn ***
into a mass burial pit in the Ponar forests
to go home

Home conjures up images of
warmth
familiar smells
laughter
security
and
peace of mind

Wilno may have been home then
but it's really
hell on earth

It's evolution in reverse
It shakes you to your very core
It makes you fear for man

So why go back you may ask

To remember
to bear witness
to be the link
to pay homage

to take care of the past

Solly Kaplinski, 1992

*grandmother and grandfather
**shot
***shit on

A World of Pains, Solly Kaplinski, 2015

Foreword

There is something strangely discomfiting when we dare explore the dark edges of memory. There in the deep well of time are places where, in times of extreme crisis, goodness and evil, loss and survival, love and hate, co-mingle in disturbing complexity.

In this thought provoking psychological thriller Solly Kaplinski artfully explores the outer edges of memory and human personality. He pushes us to ask questions about who we are, the choices we make, and how they ultimately define us.

There is much debate about the boundaries of Holocaust representation, and whether there is a need to fictionalize a history that has so much drama drawn from real life testimony. Kaplinski situates this story within events that we know happened, but about which we have little human detail or color. He does not alter the historical veracity of what occurred in those fateful and hateful times and does much to uncover the pain and their consequences. A pain which his own family endured in Lithuania and to whom he pays his own deep respects. Through his characters, he invites the reader to think in a more complex way about the disturbing implications of the Holocaust for every conscientious human being.

If your preference is for the history of the Holocaust to be black and white, that is, for the perpetrators to be evil and inhumane monsters to be written out of ordinary human history, then this may not be the book for you. If, on the other hand, you are prepared to be deeply challenged about how effortlessly the best of us can slide into mundane brutality, then what unfolds in these thought provoking pages will undoubtedly linger.

Stephen D. Smith PhD

Andrew J. and Erna Finci Viterbi Executive Director Chair,
USC Shoah
Foundation
UNESCO Chair on Genocide Education
Adjunct Professor of Religion

Los Angeles, 2015

Ponar Forest, Vilnius: October 25, 1942

"How can you do this to me, to *mein kint*, to my baby? He's ...he's not even a year old. You and I...we played together when we were children. We were in the same class in school. I even let you caress my breast. Don't you remember? I kissed you on your lips. My father tended to your parents when they were ill. My mother .... may....may she rest in peace, looked after you when you were a young child."

Rachel, gaunt and terrified, is sobbing. She clutches baby Rafael to her chest. She is naked and shivering and drops to the wet soil. She is oblivious to the gunshots, dogs barking, the screeching and wailing of the hundreds, no perhaps thousands of helpless people all around her who are facing their last moments at the hands of their brutal and merciless captors.

He looks down at her, stands firm and erect and is unmoved as she pleads desperately with him. She kisses his muddied boots. Tears are streaming down her cheeks. She puts her arm around his leg holding him tightly while at the same time trying to strengthen her grip on Rafael and to shield him. He kicks her in the face. Blood gushes out from the wound. Rachel lies in the mud, crying hysterically.

"At least… spare the child. *Hoht rahmones* – have mercy." He begins beating her violently with his rifle butt. He grabs the crying Rafael off the ground, throws him towards the pit and while the baby is hurtling through the air, he pulls the trigger. A little unsteady on his feet but encouraged by his friend Chozanda who is applauding him and has a broad grin on his face, he says, triumphantly,

"Let's go play football and drink more vodka."

Oslo: September, 1995

There is always an air of excitement at this time of the year in Oslo. Arna Bronstad, the organizing secretary of The Nobel Peace Prize Committee, is in the process of mailing out thousands of invitation letters, calling for nominations for the Nobel Peace Prize. Arna has been doing this for more than twenty years, yet every time seems like the first time.

She scans the names of people and organizations who will be receiving the letters: members of governments and international courts of law; university chancellors and professors; leaders of peace research institutes, theologians and previous Nobel Peace Prize Laureates – amongst others.

A World of Pains, Solly Kaplinski, 2015

Arna knows from past experience that the Nobel Peace Prize Committee will receive thousands of nominations by due date – postmarked no later than February 1, 1996.

The White House: Washington, January 20, 1996

The East Room, which is the largest room in the Executive Mansion of the White House, is crowded and noisy. As the President approaches the podium, the participants at the reception stand almost in unison and burst into spontaneous applause. The President, enjoying the moment, allows the applause to continue, perhaps a little longer than necessary before he gestures to them to be seated.

"No one," begins the President, "has done more for the cause of children's human rights in this country and around the world than Jonathan Varnas.

Jonathan has been a tireless and dedicated fighter for the downtrodden, for the underprivileged and for those who have been discriminated against because of their color, their sex or their religion.

Who at this distinguished gathering and around the country – and in many parts of the globe - has not heard of the Varnas Compassion Centers for Children?

Their mantra: "A children's place of safety and refuge, a shelter of loving kindness" is part of the language of expert professional care for abandoned children, for abused children, for neglected children, for children at risk – and a therapeutic model for the best there is in America for healing broken children and dysfunctional homes.

Just a few days ago, Jonathan returned from a visit to Malawi and Zimbabwe, two countries where the AIDS epidemic has left tens of thousands of orphans in its wake.

Jonathan has been at the forefront of creating child - care centers in these countries to help the children deal with their traumatic losses and to learn how to protect themselves against this scourge.

Jonathan's focus on giving equal prominence to educating parents, teachers and the clergy about their central role as loving, responsible and disciplined but fair partners in helping children, has set the bar very high in terms of best practices for children's mental and physical health and well - being.

A World of Pains, Solly Kaplinski, 2015

America is in fact a better place for his tireless and dedicated efforts to bring dignity, freedom and honor to our fellow citizens.

Jonathan serves as a role model for all that is good, noble and honest.

May I remind you all that the Presidential Medal of Freedom established by President Harry S. Truman is our highest civilian award.

It recognizes those individuals who have made and I quote 'an especially meritorious contribution to the security or national interests of the United States, world peace, cultural or other significant public or private endeavors.'

It is my pleasure and privilege to call upon Jonathan Varnas to receive this year's Presidential Medal of Freedom."

There is a roar of applause and a prolonged standing ovation as Jonathan rises from his seat and makes his way confidently and in full stride to vigorously shake the hands of the President who proceeds to place the golden star Medal of Freedom around Jonathan's neck.

Jonathan pauses for a moment to survey the crowded and dignified room.

He seems to be overwhelmed momentarily, but quickly regains his composure.

"I am deeply honored and humbled," he begins, "to stand before you Mr. President, here in the White House, in the presence of my colleagues, my friends and most important of all, my beloved wife, Sandra – or should I say Judge Sandra Rothstein, newly appointed Justice of the New York Supreme Court. Our two sons, Ruben and David, both studying law at Oxford University are also celebrating here with us. I want to first thank my partners and colleagues at our law firm, Greenberg, Goodman and Varnas, who have given me the space and the time to pursue the most noble of causes: helping our fellow man - especially those who are the most vulnerable - children. What can be more meaningful I ask you in all sincerity than to be a voice for the voiceless? While I am not a religious person, I am deeply inspired by our prophets of old and our biblical traditions, which obligate us to be of service and to be engaged in *tikun olam*: repair of the world or less grandiosely, to be engaged in acts of kindness, to be compassionate and to be committed to justice for all. Here I want to acknowledge my Rabbi, teacher and friend, Rabbi Art Brownstein of Temple Beth Israel, who schooled me in the finer details of Jewish law, Jewish history and Jewish practice over a period of many years on my path to converting to Judaism. My late mother-in-law of blessed memory, an *Eshet*

A World of Pains, Solly Kaplinski, 2015

Chayil – a woman of valor and an outstanding role model as a selfless, dedicated Jewish mother, led me down this road to becoming a Jew.

Apart from marrying her daughter, it was the best decision I ever made.

I am also especially moved by a Hebrew expression that David once brought home from his elementary school:

Kol Yisrael areivim zeh lazeh.

Loosely translated:

All Jews are responsible for each other.

As a proud American who was allowed to immigrate to this most generous and hospitable of countries during the traumatic post war years, I have adapted this mantra to embrace all my fellow Americans - as a way of expressing my deep appreciation and gratitude to those who stretched out their arms to people like me who arrived here with just the shirt on our backs – and less than a dollar in my pocket!

We were in the profound words of Emma Lazarus '...the wretched refuse... the homeless, tempest – tost...' You didn't owe us anything and yet you welcomed us with a huge heart, took us in, and made us your own.

I have never forgotten that.

Kol Yisrael areivim zeh lazeh: the Hebrew word *areivim* means in a sense – guarantee.

Those of us in the legal fraternity know only too well what it means to be a guarantor. For me who has worked with my colleagues and friends in the field of human rights all these years, it means standing up for others. It means protecting and defending those who need it the most. It means shouting from the barricades at those who do harm to others.

You do what my family calls a *mitzvah*, a good deed, simply because it's the right thing to do, not because you expect a reward for your efforts.

If there is one person I need to thank more than anyone else for this recognition but more importantly for the work that I have been privileged to be doing, it's my beloved wife Sandra. When I arrived in this country raw off the boat, together with Sandra and her late mother, Sima of blessed memory, I was a *griner* as they colloquially say to anyone who knows from nothing!

I learnt first-hand what being a parent is by seeing how hard Sima worked and the sacrifices she made, for example, purchasing almost nothing for herself, to enable Sandra to attend university and finish law school.

Fate brought us together in Vilnius. It was to quote a Yiddish word: *bashert* – destined to be, a match made in heaven, divinely inspired! Sandra, together with her mother, taught me everything there is to know about the Jewish faith, about life in general and how important it is to be a mensch: a person who lives his life with dignity, sensitivity and respect for others.

Sandra, my darling, I have no words to express my love, admiration and deepest respect for you.

Ruben and David: how proud we both are of your outstanding achievements! As a young person growing up in war torn Lithuania - and you know it's always been too painful for me to talk about my past, I delight in the fact that both of you have such an excellent start in life. You have had the good fortune to grow up in a free, democratic country where all doors are open for you and where the only barriers to your success are the limits of your imagination.

In closing, my friends, I find it so hard to believe that from such spartan and humble beginnings in a small *shtetl* in Kaunas, Lithuania, a tiny village which is no longer found on a map, I am the recipient of this Medal of Freedom which has also been awarded to people I have so admired, including former President Ronald Reagan, Elie Wiesel, Martin Luther King Junior and especially, Mother Theresa. Only in America!

Finally, Mr. President, let me thank you in particular for this award.

While it may have my name attached to it, as your wife has said – it takes a village! We are all in this together.

Your encouragement and support gives us the emotional strength and psychological stamina and emboldens us in our joint and determined efforts to confront the challenges of our time, especially protecting the weak, the frail and those who are discriminated against, and to be an advocate for the vulnerable and the weak and the unprotected in our midst."

Everyone in the crowded room stands once again to congratulate Jonathan as he makes his way amidst the hugging, the backslapping and the handshakes back to his table. Sandra gives him a warm embrace, as do the Varnas boys.

Jonathan is overcome with emotion and breaks down when Gene Goodman, his close friend and law partner says, "If only your parents were alive to see this - how proud they would be!"

A World of Pains, Solly Kaplinski, 2015

The offices of Greenberg, Goodman and Varnas, Manhattan: January 23, 1996

Don Greenberg, Gene Goodman and Jonathan Varnas studied law together and graduated at the same time from New York University.

They became close friends.

The law firm Greenberg, Goodman and Varnas was established in the early 1950's focusing specifically on corporate law and criminal defense.

United by their wish to stay small and focused, they resisted the temptation initially to grow their firm, despite great legal successes with high profile clients and a growing reputation for providing stellar service.

On the tenth anniversary of the founding of their law practice, they moved reluctantly from their cramped quarters on the Lower East Side to downtown Manhattan to more spacious offices.

Symbolically, the change of address reflected their upwardly mobile status - and respect and admiration from their clients who remained loyal to them over many years.

Their law offices, while not austere, remained modest but homely and especially designed to make their clients feel comfortable and at ease. Jonathan had insisted that there was no need to be flamboyant and ostentatious even though they could well afford it.

The firm's ten partners are seated around a U - shaped table in the boardroom for their weekly meeting. On the table are pitchers of water and glasses as well as several bottles of red wine – a first for the partners' meetings. At the back of the room are facilities for making coffee and a few trays of cookies.

Gene downs a glass of water and calls the meeting to order.

"Firstly," he says, clearing his throat, "I would like to congratulate Jonathan again on being deservedly awarded the Presidential Medal of Freedom. Not only has this brought great honor to Jonathan and his family, but also to our firm. Jonathan, I feel privileged to call you my partner and especially my friend. We have known each other for more than forty years and have enjoyed good times along with some low points.

This award has only served to strengthen our relationship and all of us at Greenberg, Goodman and Varnas.

A World of Pains, Solly Kaplinski, 2015

My dear colleagues, please fill your glasses, let's say a hearty *mazeltov* and congratulations, and toast a *le' hayim to* Jonathan. To life! Cheers!"

Everyone duly stands to salute Jonathan and to wish him well. "Now, let's get down to the urgent business of the day.

Jonathan, I apologize for bringing you so quickly back to reality. I know that your preference is not to take on cases involving child abuse.

You have always said that your feelings overcome you in such situations, but at this stage, the firm is stretched to capacity. Furthermore, this is going to be a sensational case and fodder for the tabloids.

I need someone who will be levelheaded, stay calm and fend off the media in what will for sure be a high profile case.

Frankly, your outstanding work, your good name and reputation, your quality involvement in the field of children's human rights, and your substantial accomplishments all bring tremendous gravitas and legitimacy to the defense.

I am referring to the breaking Jackson case which has already made the headlines in this morning's New York Times."

"Gene, I only caught snatches of it on the car radio this morning on my way to work. Please give me more details."

Gene drains the remaining wine in his glass and speaks, as is his habit, from a standing position. "Amanda Jackson, the famous movie star, who won an Oscar a few years ago, has laid a charge against her husband, the basketball star, Stevie Wolfman for allegedly killing their infant child, Moe. Apparently, the three of them were returning by car from a brief winter vacation and an argument ensued which became violent."

Gene pauses for a moment to clear his throat.

"He accused her of having an affair with a close friend. She denied it. He questioned whether in fact the baby was his. He became verbally abusive to her while she was driving. It is not clear what exactly happened next: he may have been under the influence of alcohol. He grabbed the infant from the baby seat in the back. She stopped the car to try to restrain him. He opened up the front door of the car and threw the infant out of the car with such force that passersby heard a loud thump as the child crashed against a telegraph pole. A witness to this dastardly deed saw the wires quiver from the impact.

Wolfman is being charged with second-degree murder. And since we have represented him in the past, he has approached us to act as his lawyers."

A World of Pains, Solly Kaplinski, 2015

There is a silence in the room, almost uncomfortably too long. Jonathan is fidgeting in his chair gazing into the distance.

"Gene, let me think about this for a day or two. My knee jerk reaction is to say no. I get too emotionally involved in cases of this kind and as you intimated, this is sometimes to the detriment of my better judgment and professional expertise."

With the formal business concluded, the partners stand and leave the room.

The Varnas residence, New Jersey: January 23, 1996

The Varnas home, a well lived in and comfortable two-storey Tudor revival style with a step pitch side gable roof and semi-hexagonal bay windows, was bought by Jonathan and Sandra in 1960 – thanks to a very successful settlement of a prominent law case won by Jonathan, the lead attorney.

Originally built in the early 1900's, the Varnas's fell in love with it at first sight when they were house searching and while both Jonathan and Sandra were extremely hard working in their professional spheres, they loved nothing better than to spend dinner time together at home – preferably with the boys as well.

Very little was allowed to impinge on this daily quality time. But following the partners' meeting that day, most unusually for Jonathan and to Sandra's dismay, he skipped dinner, pleading a sudden and inexplicable sheer exhaustion.

His sleep that night is a restless one. He tosses and turns and cries out as if pained. Sandra wakes him up from his disturbed sleep. He is sweating and breathing heavily.

"Jonathan, what's upsetting you? It sounds like an awful nightmare. Can you remember what you were dreaming about?" Jonathan is unable to recall a thing. He has to change his pajamas since they are soaked through.

In the morning, they sit down to breakfast in the well-lit kitchen. No reference is made to the night before. There is light banter between Ruben and David, who are soon to return to Oxford. Sandra talks briefly about the case that is currently before the Supreme Court, dealing with the burning of the American flag, which involves freedom of speech.

A discussion ensues around the table on what if any limits there are or should be to this sacred principle and value, which is enshrined in the Constitution. The boys weigh in and say that there should be no such limits, that all are protected by the law, that if one imposes restraints, it will drive potential recalcitrants underground.

A World of Pains, Solly Kaplinski, 2015

Better to keep everything open and transparent even if it becomes unpleasant. There should be no censorship. "Sunlight", quoting U.S. Supreme Court Justice Louis Brandeis "is the best disinfectant."

"Jonathan," says Sandra, "I wonder how my parents or yours would have responded to this question."

"I must admit that I have mixed feelings on this issue," replies Jonathan. "On the one hand every person should be free to say whatever he or she likes – even burn our flag, but everyone has to be subject to the laws of the country.

If what is said borders on hate, discrimination, slander, libel and essentially threatens the lives of others, that's where I draw the line, that's when our laws have to kick in and protect our citizens.

Protection of human life has to be our number one, sacrosanct and absolute non-negotiable principle and value. If this principle had been in operation when you and I were growing up in Kaunas and Vilnius, things would have been a whole lot better for our fellow citizens.

The Holocaust and the tragedy of the World War Two may have been averted."

Jonathan excuses himself from the table; he needs to get ready for work.

While shaving in the bathroom, Jonathan is deep in thought about the Wolfman tragedy and he has mixed feelings about whether to accept this case. He is not keen. He knows it will be overly stressful, that he will probably not be able to give of his best.

He is staring at himself in the mirror when suddenly and without warning, out of the corner of his eye, he sees a blurry image of what appears to be the contours of a young infant - and then it is gone. He turns around to see whether perhaps one of the boys has been fooling around, as they often do. But no one is there. He thinks nothing of it as he drives to work.

Although the day passes uneventfully, Jonathan is battling to get through it. He is simply exhausted from the night before and for the first time since he can remember, he leaves the office early and as soon as he arrives home, falls asleep almost immediately while sitting in front of the television. All the channels are focused on the now sensational Jackson case.

Sandra inadvertently wakes up Jonathan a few hours later as she walks through the front door.

He stands up to embrace her.

"My darling, I need to tell you that I have been having this unusual and frankly, a little scary dream," Jonathan begins.

"Please tell me about it."

"I know this may sound strange but I saw my own eyes in my dream, as if my eyes were staring at me, watching intensely what I am doing, almost as if they were spying on me. Can it be possible? Moreover, sometimes my eyes would smile at me and sometimes they would be glaring, almost venomous. And on occasion, my eyes in my dream were shut.

This is very strange. I rarely remember my dreams yet this one is so vivid, so real. I don't know what to make of this." Jonathan dabs away the beads of sweat on his forehead.

Sandra is somewhat taken aback by the seeming bizarreness of the dream but tries not to show it.

"I remember," she says casually "when I did a few courses in psychology at college, we studied Sigmund Freud rather superficially and his interpretation of dreams. I didn't think much of it at the time and didn't attribute significance to his theories although what has stayed with me is his stressing that dreams are somehow connected to unconscious wish fulfillment. What we dream about is what we actually aspire towards.

My gut feeling is that this isn't something about which you need to be overly concerned. However, since you seem to be anxious, which is not like you my love, let me speak to one of my colleagues Julie Morris, who as you know is a psychologist.

We collaborated on some legal cases in the past. Perhaps she can shed some light on this. I'll give her a call after dinner. I am sure she will allay your anxiety."

Speaking with Julie

After exchanging the usual pleasantries, Sandra got straight to the point. "Julie, I am sure it's nothing serious but Jonathan has had what I consider a somewhat bizarre dream. Normally I would not call you to discuss this but the dream follows a very restless night. He also came home early from the office, which is out of character for him. In his dream, he could see his eyes staring at him as if they were watching him.

Now I know Jonathan is not normally paranoid but while I am not overly concerned, this is somewhat disconcerting. He also mentioned that sometimes his eyes in his dream were shut."

"Sandra, is there something which he is worried about, something which is bothering him? I saw him last with you at the wonderful function where he received the Presidential Medal of Honor. What a dignified, impressive and moving event! He seemed to be on top of the world.

A World of Pains, Solly Kaplinski, 2015

Rumor also has it by the way that there is a move afoot to submit his name as a nominee for the Nobel Prize!"

"I have also heard vaguely about this. And what a great honor it would be Julie. I am of course very excited for him at the prospect but I am keeping my emotions in check! My Jonathan is not in this for the accolades.

Regarding your question whether there's anything worrying him, other than the restless night, there's nothing untoward that I am aware of. He has been on a high these last few days and we are savoring the moment. But tell me Julie, what do you think? Should I or we attach any significance to this or should we let it go, which is what I am inclined to do?"

"Obviously without seeing Jonathan and discussing this with him in more detail, I have to be cautious in my interpretation which will be, as you can understand, superficial.

In brief, Jonathan's dream while not rare is unusual. Put very simply and without going into detail, eyes are often seen as the window to the soul, as an opening to one's inner self and when they appear in a dream, it's as if they are showing one what's going on underneath or very close to the surface. We often are unaware in our daily interactions, conversations and behaviors of why we do the things we do and what motivates us.

Perhaps I can explain it this way Sandra: If someone were to do a sketch of our behaviors, it would resemble an iceberg. What we are aware and conscious of behaviorally is the small part of the iceberg that protrudes out of the water, the tip that is sometimes barely visible.

The vast bulk of the iceberg, which is below the water, is the metaphorical equivalent of our unconscious which according to our friend Sigmund, influences our behavior and over which we have very little if any knowledge and control.

It is possible therefore that with Jonathan, there are things bubbling below the surface that are somehow affecting his present behaviors.

Before we take this any further however, I suggest that you ask him if all is well, if there are things at work that may be anxiety provoking.

I would be happy to meet him or refer him to somebody who can help.

Sandra, I also know from our various conversations and by reputation that Jonathan is a type-A personality, a perfectionist who is extremely competitive, with a strong work ethic and while he is demanding of others, he is especially demanding of himself.

A World of Pains, Solly Kaplinski, 2015

Maybe he is pushing himself too much? Perhaps he needs to slow down, take some time out? Between the both of you, I know how busy your schedules are. I think both of you need to find the time to mellow and chill out and to enjoy some quality time together."

Sandra says with a sigh, "That would be wonderful. I don't remember the last time we took a holiday together.

Our neighbors and close friends – you know them: Neil and Orly Berman have just returned from a vacation in South Africa and highly recommended that we visit Cape Town, which they say is a place of stunning and breathtaking beauty. Knowing my passion for the sea, Orly especially mentioned the pristine Muizenberg beach. That would be a dream come true!

But truth be told, Jonathan has been burying himself in his work as if there is no tomorrow – and that's been the pattern of his – and our lives ever since I can remember. It's frenetic at times.

It's as if he is on a roller coaster and doesn't want to or is unable to get off. It seems as if work is almost an escape for him..."

Sandra decides not to pursue this with Jonathan in the meantime, hoping that this unusual occurrence is a one off event.

The offices of Greenberg, Goodman and Varnas, Manhattan: March 13, 1996

Jonathan takes on the Jackson v. Wolfman case and begins to immerse himself in the details – almost to the exclusion of everything else. Sitting at his desk poring over the various documents however, he battles to stay focused, and finds himself having to take numerous breaks. He has to force himself to continue studying the various texts.

Jonathan is horrified and repulsed by what Wolfman has done, begins to feel nauseous and at one point rushes to the washroom to throw up. "How could he do such an awful thing to a young, defenseless infant?" he repeatedly asks himself. Moreover, knowing how juries tend to react in such high profile cases – more often than not being antagonistic to the accused, Jonathan believes he is facing an almost impossible situation.

Clearly, no one can condone this barbaric crime but in grappling with this awful tragedy, Jonathan believes strongly that if being under the influence of alcohol is a possible factor, a mitigating circumstance leading to Wolfman's diminished responsibility, he would at least have some opening to argue vigorously and with credibility for a lesser jail sentence. Guilty for sure but no malice aforethought.

A World of Pains, Solly Kaplinski, 2015

Jonathan also knows that the star image of Wolfman, who has an outstanding record on the basketball court and has just signed a new multimillion-dollar contract with his team, will not wash with the jury given the magnitude of the crime and the outcry of the public.

In addition, while all are innocent before the law until proven otherwise, Jonathan has already come to terms with the fact that in the court of public opinion, his client is to all intents and purposes already guilty. The media and the tabloids especially are having a field day and the public are clearly on the side of Amanda, the aggrieved and anguished mother, who has suffered an unbearable and tragic loss. People are baying for blood and relish the prospect of yet another star falling from grace. Jonathan decides to visit Wolfman.

Rikers: March 20, 1996

In 1932, the city of New York opened a jail for men on the island of Rikers. Today, a complex of ten jails holds more than 12,000 inmates at a cost of approximately $167,000 annually per prisoner. Local offenders are housed there because they could not afford bail or were not granted bail by a judge. Wolfman falls into this latter category.

Wolfman is escorted in chains by a thickset, emotionless security guard into a bare room, dimly lit. He sits at a table opposite Jonathan. They stare at each other in silence for a few moments.

"Stevie, I'm going to get straight to the point here. No niceties here or being politically correct. I am taking off my lawyer's hat. What for heaven's sake got into you? How could you do this? How am I going to defend you? You must surely know that only a handful of people are taking your side.

Looking at the letters to the press and the talkbacks on the internet and watching the talking heads on TV, despite your superlative talents as one of America's top basketball players and your overwhelming popularity in the last few years, even your strongest and most outspoken fans – and I count myself amongst them, are finding it very difficult, if not impossible to stand by you. How are we going to move forward on this? Give me some ammunition to defend you.

Tell me for God's sake, what happened?"

Stevie gets up from the table, pacing the small room frantically from side to side, unable to say a word, his hands over his ears as if to shut out the world.

The sounds of the chains around his ankles piercingly scrape the cement floor.

A World of Pains, Solly Kaplinski, 2015

After a few minutes, he returns to his chair and sits down staring at the floor. There are tears in his eyes. He struggles to regain his composure and tries to speak but can't get the words out. Jonathan stretches his hand out to grasp his and holds it tight.

"Jonathan, this is the first time we are meeting so...slow down. You ...you don't know me at all. You need to understand that I...I am in shock and depression about what happened. I am filled with remorse and regret. If only I could turn back the clock ... I killed a child, possibly my own flesh and blood, my own child," he begins to sob. "You...you... will never know what it's like to kill a child. Never.... especially your own child. Nothing justifies my action, my behavior. Nothing.

I know that I was drinking heavily and got into a slanging match with Amanda because I suspected her of infidelity. We were arguing about having DNA tests to establish my paternity. The next thing I knew I was in an unbelievable and uncontrollable rage – probably fueled by the booze."

Jonathan is, in retrospect, embarrassed and ashamed at his uncharacteristic outburst – and his lack of empathy. This is so unlike him.

He needs to get a grip on himself.

He is also taken aback by Stevie's turn of phrase, by his articulate deliberation and by what seemed to be genuine feelings of remorse and upset.

Jonathan's stereotype of sportsmen as stuttering, limited and inept individuals with poor social skills but gigantic egos was certainly taking a huge knock. He felt a degree of sympathy with his client that was unexpected.

"Stevie, let me firstly apologize to you for my harsh and intemperate words. I feel bad about that. Is there anything else I need to know?"

"What I did was inexcusable and I need to be severely punished. To take baby Moe and throw him out of the car ..." the words trail off as he breaks down, "...is...is... something I ....will take to the grave with me.

This is a stain that will stay with me for the rest of my life. Whatever good I have done in my life, whatever pleasure and joy I have brought to my fans means nothing. I am destroyed. I am ruined. I don't know how I will live with myself. I deserve the electric chair."

Jonathan puts his arms around his client, hugs him and leaves. On the way out, he speaks with the chief warder and tells him that his client needs the help of a psychologist and that he should be put on 24-hour daily suicide watch.

A World of Pains, Solly Kaplinski, 2015

Driving in his car back to the office he plays back the scene with Stevie and marvels at what he has just witnessed – a broken and contrite person but sober enough to recognize the gravity of his situation and to take full responsibility for his actions, fully understanding the consequences and the punishment to which he may be subjected.

Jonathan now has to make a decision about how best to defend his client. Yes, his client is culpable, and yes, there cannot be any justification for what he did and yes, the law has to take its course. However, this cannot be about vengeance. Furthermore, Stevie, despite the scarlet letter that he will forever have burnt on his forehead, still has the capacity to be a useful citizen and constructive member of society.

Jonathan feels the heavy weight of responsibility to act to the best of his ability on his client's behalf and to ensure that despite the noise and the harsh glare of the media spotlight that is shining on the Jackson family around the clock, his client gets a fair trial.

Jonathan still has some distance to reach the office and turns on the car radio. There is a panel of agitated and hysterical speakers dissecting the horror of baby Moe's death. Jonathan switches off the radio immediately.

Without warning, he feels strong pains in his chest and a shortness of breath. He has to swerve swiftly to avoid an oncoming car. He pulls over to the side of the road to calm himself. He notices that his hands are cold and sweaty and is conscious of his heart beating loudly and rapidly.

Ponar Forest, Vilnius: October 26, 1942

When Yonas awakes the next day following his drunken stupor, his mind is a blank. It's almost as if the day before never happened. Other than having faint recollections about the chaos and noise, crying, gunshots and bodies lying on top of each other in deep pits, he struggles to remember what transpired. He knew he had taken a train to Ponar to see what was happening there with the Jewish scum. He had heard that they were getting their just desserts and he felt a sense of satisfaction.

Yonas was born in Kaunas, Lithuania in 1924 to poor, illiterate parents who had already borne three children before him. They lived from hand to mouth relying on the generosity of the local church and their neighbors to survive. His parents

A World of Pains, Solly Kaplinski, 2015

were reasonably civil to the Braudes who lived opposite them and the family were always treated by Dr. Braude at no cost.

While Yonas himself was in the same class in elementary school as their youngest daughter, Rachel, and they seemed to get along, the talk at home was always about "those Jews who have everything, Christ killers, about how they cheat and lie to get ahead and how they are the enemies of the Lithuanian people."

His father always used to ramble on especially after a few bottles of vodka about "how evil the Jews are and that…the best Jew is a dead one! The Jews are our misfortune - *Die Juden sind unser Unglück!*" he would proclaim periodically.

When Yonas was all of four years old, whenever he saw Dr. Braude, he would always say, "Hello Jew" which Braude ignored.

Around Easter time, the children were always forbidden to wonder too close to the Braude home for fear that one of them would be kidnapped and murdered and that their blood would be used as part of the ingredients for the strange bread that Jews ate at that time of the year.

Yonas's parents were deliriously happy when the Braudes decided to move to Vilnius. Dr. Braude was offered a partnership in a local medical practice.

Yonas's reflections on the past are interrupted by the constant wailing and screaming of trainloads of Jews who are arriving and are being marched into Ponar.

Some lines from one of his favorite books at school also come to mind as he observes those whining and painful Jews:

'The alien Jew, that scurvy knave.
His nomad soul finds nowhere rest,
Everywhere he's just a pest.

Four centuries have come and gone,
Ahasuerus crops up everywhere
Now in Hamburg, next Berlin,
In Denmark and in Danzig too.
Dresden, Paris have seen that Jew.

Believe me, children, it is quite clear,
Ahasuerus haunts us still
Under the skin of every Jew.

Now, children, keep a good look out
Whenever you see a Jew about.
The Jew creeps round, a regular fox,
Keep your eyes open, or you'll be on the rocks.'

A World of Pains, Solly Kaplinski, 2015

Yonas remembers going with his father to celebrate a family wedding in late June of the previous year. Soon after the marriage ceremony, the father of the bride invited some of the guests to attend a special event as part of the celebrations.

They all walked merrily to the nearby Lietukus garage where a crowd had gathered. There was a lot of noise and commotion, and loud wails and screams. Yonas had to strain himself in order to see what was going on - and to try to understand why the people around him were so happy and why they were applauding furiously.

At first, he was amazed to see fellow Lithuanians with iron bars, wooden sticks and water pipes beating unarmed men, women and children.

Their cries of pain and humiliation pierced the heavens. And the more they cried, the more the bystanders laughed and shouted - egging on the perpetrators.

His curiosity piqued, Yonas pushed his way through the wall of men and women to the front of the crowd where he witnessed two elderly men with long side curls and a few children doubled over on their hands and knees.

They were being forced to collect garbage and feces with their hands before being savagely beaten with long iron bars - and then lying motionless in the yard.

The onlookers – men and women, some with babes in their arms or children perched on their shoulders to get a better view, were cheering on the killers and periodically breaking into fits of laughter. Yonas also joined in whistling, shouting, and vigorously clapping his hands.

One of the young men known as the "Death Dealer" who had just killed a victim with a wooden club took a bow and posed for a photograph, standing on a pile of dead bodies with a jubilant expression on his face.

"Encore! Encore!" cried the crowd deliriously.

When there were no more Jews left to butcher and the violence eventually subsided, someone who appeared to be the leader of the group whipped out a harmonica from his pocket and played the Lithuanian national anthem. Everyone joined in enthusiastically.

Lietuva, Tėvyne mūsų,
Tu didvyrių žeme,
Iš praeities Tavo sūnūs
Te stiprybę semia.
Tegul Tavo vaikai eina
Vien takais dorybės,
Tegul dirba Tavo naudai

A World of Pains, Solly Kaplinski, 2015

Ir žmonių gėrybei.

Tegul saulė Lietuvoj

Tamsumas prašalina,

Ir šviesa, ir tiesa

Mūs žingsnius telydi.

Tegul meilė Lietuvos

Dega mūsų širdyse,

Vardan tos, Lietuvos

Vienybė težydi!

Lithuania, our homeland,

Land of heroes!

Let your sons draw their strength

From our past experience.

Let your children always follow

Only roads of virtue,

May your own, mankind's well-being

Be the goals they work for.

May the sun above our land

Banish darkening clouds around

Light and truth all along

Guide our steps forever.

May the love of Lithuania
Brightly burn in our hearts.
For the sake of this land,
Let unity blossom!

Overall, sixty-eight defenseless Jews were murdered on that glorious sunny summer's day in the 'land of heroes'.

Yonas looks again at the scene around him in Ponar; he is unmoved by the plight of those *zhids*, those fucking Jews being marched to the pits other than a sense of *schadenfreude* that his next-door Jewish neighbors were whisked out of their homes in the dead of night never to be seen again. Yonas knows there will be rich pickings from their homes.

In truth, Yonas is not enthusiastic about returning to his home in Kaunas after his two days in Ponar. There is no warmth in the home and his parents are constantly bickering and at each other's throats. In addition, being the youngest in the family, Yonas is constantly on the receiving end of taunts and fisticuffs by his siblings. His options, however, are limited. He has at the age of eighteen a meager elementary school education, no job skills and very few prospects.

Feeling that he has nothing to lose, Yonas decides that rather than going back to Kaunas, he will meet with a distant family relative, Jurgis Kanas, a highly respected and experienced lawyer who had moved to Vilnius in the late summer of 1940 from the Western Lithuanian town of Zezmariai.

Yonas had heard that Kanas was looking for an assistant to do menial chores and run errands.

Kanas and Yonas: January 7, 1943

Kanas is regarded by all who know him as a person of integrity and devoted to helping his many clients from all stations of life. A bachelor in his sixties, his life revolves almost exclusively around his extremely busy practice.

Kanas's cluttered and dimly lit office is in a modest block near the high street in Vilnius. Files are stacked everywhere including on Kanas's desk, in various bookcases and even on the floor.

Yonas on his first day at work notices that the offices next to Kanas's are boarded off. He thinks nothing of it as he studies an inscription placed prominently on the wall behind framed glass:

"..to thine own self be true,

And it must follow, as the night the day,

Thou cans't not be false to any man."

He asks Kanas what this means.

"These words come from my favorite author and poet, William Shakespeare."

"Who is he?" asks Yonas.

"Shakespeare is probably the greatest writer in the English language. I studied his books when I was at University.

This sentence comes from his play Hamlet, written more than three hundred years ago.

Yonas, this is an amazing and very sad story, a tragedy about Hamlet, a Danish Prince who takes revenge on his uncle Claudius who murdered his father, the King of Denmark.

Prince Hamlet then becomes King of Denmark and marries the King's widow, his mother!

Yes, I can see by the expression on your face – a most unusual, even bizarre story!"

"And what about the meaning of that sentence behind the glass frame?"

A World of Pains, Solly Kaplinski, 2015

"More than anything else in my life both personally and professionally, I have tried and not always successfully I must admit, to be honest with others - and myself. This is not always easy and straightforward.

Let me also add that I have been guided in this by one of the Ten Commandments that were given by God to the Jews, 'Thou shalt not bear false witness.' This to me is what the principles of justice and fair play are based on.

One should not tell lies about other people. One should not slander them. It has been difficult at times to live up to this principle of truthfulness and especially today with what's happening in our country."

Yonas is shocked at these words.

"I don't understand what you have said about the Jews. I have always seen them as cruel, vicious and dangerous and people who can't be trusted.

Those Jews, those bastard communists have brought ruin to our country. They are the cause of all the world's problems, those bloodsuckers who crucified our Lord Jesus."

Yonas is now in full flight and raises his voice. "They always think that they are smarter than we are and they are obsessed with money.

They have long noses because the air is free! I hate them, those *judenscheisse*. They are *untermenschen*, subhuman. I remember a poem that I had to memorize at school:

'A devil goes through the land,
it's the Jew, well known to us
as a murderer of peoples,
a race defiler, a child's horror in all lands!

Corrupting our youth
stands him in good stead.
He wants all peoples dead.
Stay away from every Jew
and happiness will come to you.'

Kanas, his eyes closed, adjusts his tie, sits quietly for a few moments deep in thought, stands tiredly to retrieve almost in slow motion a book from one of his bookshelves, dusts it off with his hand and opens it up.

"Yonas, I mentioned Shakespeare's words to you earlier for one simple reason: he gives us the words to describe what we are feeling and thinking.

A World of Pains, Solly Kaplinski, 2015

He empowers us to understand what motivates people, what drives them and why they - we - behave in the way we do. He says it better than all of us, so let me quote a few more sentences from this play in my hands called 'The Merchant of Venice.'

One of his most famous characters Shylock, a Jew who is agitated and distressed by the manner in which Christians are treating him, cries out:

'... *He has disgrac'd me and*
hind'red me half a million,
laugh'd at my losses,
mock'd at gains,
scorned my nation,
thwarted my bargains,
cooled my friends,
heated mine enemies.
And what's his reason?

I am a Jew.

Hath not a Jew eyes? Hath not a Jew hands, organs, dimensions, senses, affections, passions fed with the same food, hurt with the same weapons, subject to the same diseases, healed by the same means, warmed and cooled by the same winter and summer, as a Christian is?

If you prick us, do we not bleed? If you tickle us, do we not laugh? If you poison us, do we not die?'

In other words Yonas, Jews are not different from anyone else. Yes, there are some rotten apples, some bad ones just like there are amongst our people. I don't have to tell you what's happening just outside my office and our homes. However, there also many who are exceptionally decent, honest, and hard working. If you want to work with me, I will not tolerate at all the awful and insulting words that have come out of your mouth."

Yonas is seemingly mesmerized by Kanas's words and is unable to respond.

"All my life I have tried hard to be unprejudiced in my dealings with others, not to be influenced by a person's religion or race, to treat everyone fairly and respectfully and without prejudice. This little sculpture on my desk with a blindfolded woman holding the scales of justice reminds me every day that the law is and must be always blind to one's religion, race and gender.

Now I know that the newspaper you have in your hand, that rag you read so religiously every day, *Naujoji Lietuva*, constantly refer to Jews as parasites and exploiters and that Hitler's Europe must be cleansed of Jews, but what you have said, Yonas, goes against everything I stand for and believe. You are putting a knife into my heart. I am so deeply pained and ashamed of your attitude and behavior."

Yonas looks away and bows his head in sorrow.

"I am sure you saw the offices next door mine, that they were boarded up. They belonged to someone for whom I had the deepest respect and who was my partner: Advocate Jacob Rothstein. I saw with my own eyes how he was picked up off the street and molested by some people that I unfortunately know, and taken to who knows where. I fear for him. I don't know if he is still alive. And his only crime? That he is a Jew. And I... I have stood by silently doing nothing. Not raising my voice, not protesting and enabling those savages to destroy innocent people. I have not kept true to my guiding principles that have steered me all my life. And do you know why? I am scared, I am petrified – and I am so ashamed. I do not have the courage. I am a broken man." Kanas breaks down and finds it difficult to regain his composure.

After some time has passed, he says,

"You have a choice, Yonas. You are like family and that is why I am prepared to take a chance on you. But I need to know that despite everything you may have been taught or heard and saw in your home, in the church, on the radio or amongst your friends or even at school, you are prepared to turn over a new leaf, to make a fresh start, to see the world through different eyes. Are you prepared to do that?"

Oslo: February, 1996

More than 200 different nominations (including thirty-three organizations) for the Nobel Peace Prize have been received although there are many more letters since some candidates have been nominated by more than one person or organization. The Nobel Foundation statutes restrict disclosure of information about the nominees and nominators as well as the investigation process for fifty years.

Arna Bronstad, the organizing secretary of the Nobel Peace Prize Committee scans the impressive list of nominees. Her initial impressions are that there appear to be a few obvious choices as well as some who will probably be ruled out because they are too controversial.

She reminds herself however that one can never make truly accurate predictions about the eventual winner. Nominated members who did not receive the Nobel Peace Prize include Joseph Stalin, Benito Mussolini and Adolf Hitler. Yasser Arafat joined the elite ranks. Winston Churchill did not. Neither did Mahatma Gandhi.

Arna recalled Arafat's Nobel Prize speech where he spoke about the 'peace of the brave' and one of her colleagues sitting next to her who was shocked at his selection whispering to her that "...he really means piss on their graves."

The Nobel Committee's five members appointed by the Norwegian Parliament will narrow the candidates down to a short list – not more than twenty candidates. They also have the discretion to add their own nominees.

A small group of Norwegian University professors will spend a few months engaged in comprehensive research reports on each candidate.

How the final selections are made will remain a mystery but before the actual announcement is made in October, there will be plenty of speculation and wild guesses in the media about possible candidates.

The offices of Greenberg, Goodman and Varnas, Manhattan: May 5, 1996

Jonathan is poring over documents and is deep in thought. He barely notices Gene who walks into the room.

"How is the Wolfman case progressing?"

"We are still at the initial stages Gene. This is proving to be complicated but as you know in this firm, we have a never-say-die attitude. I am determined that we will give it our best efforts."

"I know this case is emotionally difficult for you Jonathan, given your dedication to fighting for the rights of defenselessness and innocent children, and for them to be acknowledged as sacred and precious human beings."

"Gene, I have this little plaque on my cluttered desk which always faces me and is a constant reminder of what I am trying to accomplish. I am not sure if you have seen it so let me turn it around so you can see the words:

'What a powerful effect on the sad life of a child,

would be the memory of that person –

perhaps the only one –

who showed kindness, understanding and respect

A World of Pains, Solly Kaplinski, 2015

In a world where cruelty has become the norm
the child's future life and sense of himself
could take a different course
knowing there was one person
who would not fail him.'

Janusz Korczak

Korczak is the major inspiration for my involvement in human rights work. He was, as you know, the Director of two orphanages in the Warsaw Ghetto, an internationally renowned doctor, writer, educator, philosopher and pioneer for children's rights.

Despite having a number of opportunities to leave war- torn Europe and despite being pressurized to do so by prominent people around the world, he chose not to abandon the children in his care but rather to accompany almost two hundred of them to his and their deaths in Treblinka.

For me, he is the ultimate role model who I have tried humbly to emulate in my efforts to improve the lives of vulnerable and at risk children.

My Rabbi taught me a Talmudic verse that I have never forgotten:

'He who has saved a life - it's as if he has saved a whole universe.'

While it is too late for little Moe Wolfman who has so violently lost his life, bringing him justice at the very least, gives us the strength to continue the fight, and to let him rest in peace. Gene, I know that's a long answer to your question about how we are progressing!"

Gene gets up to leave. He is concerned that even though the air conditioner in the office is keeping the room cool, Jonathan is sweating profusely and that his shirt is drenched but he decides not to say anything about it.

Kanas and Yonas: 1943 -1944

Under Kanas's watchful eye, Yonas begins to see the world through a new lens. He not only becomes a hardworking, dedicated and loyal assistant to Kanas, he also begins to appreciate what it means to be a lawyer with high professional standards and a person dedicated to fighting for the rights of all his clients - from the very poor to the affluent.

Yonas sees how rigorously Kanas prepares for his cases, the research he undertakes so thoroughly to guide him through the intricacies of the law, and above all, the respect and dignity he accords his clients - no matter what crimes they are accused of and regardless of their status.

Kanas, for all his knowledge of the law, knows however that no matter how clearly understood the legal system presumes to protect the innocent and the downtrodden, it is in the hearts of men and women, that one's ultimate rights and freedom will be protected. And in the Lithuania of 1941 - 1944, where tens of thousands of Jews are being rounded up off the streets and from their apartments and sent to be exterminated in the Ponar forest which is situated less than 10 miles from the center of Vilnius, the legal system to all intents and purposes, has collapsed and broken down. Moreover, there is no one, it seems, who is prepared to stand up to this ruthless killing machine. What is especially painful for him to observe is the local citizens who themselves have been involved in the brutality and slaughter not only of random Jews but their very own neighbors.

Kanas cannot fathom how it is possible for neighbors who have been friendly for years, maybe generations, who have eaten in each other's kitchens, whose children went to school together, who consoled and mourned together, who shared gossip and intimate secrets, who screwed each other's wives, who were comrades from military service, fellows of the same fire brigade, footballers in the same team, old cronies, drinking buddies, to suddenly turn on their friends and become savage, unfeeling and merciless murderers.

And these killers came from all strata: from manual workers and farmers to teachers and members of the clergy, from doctors and chemists to engineers and lawyers, from the exceedingly poor to the very wealthy, from the lower and middle classes to the intellectual elite.

All over Lithuania from the smallest village to the largest cities, starting with the cultural and spiritual elite, all Jews were singled out for death – even before the German army arrived. And in many situations, Jews were murdered with prominent people looking on and cheering - including mayors of cities, school principals, church officials and other highly respected dignitaries.

Kanas had heard from one of his clients in Slobodka where the first pogroms were committed that Rabbi Ossovski, who was the Chief Rabbi of Slobodka, was murdered while he was sitting and studying the *Talmud,* the vast collection of Jewish laws and Jewish wisdom.

One of the leaders of the pogrom decapitated him and exhibited his head on the front windowsill of his home. His headless body was found in another room slumped in a chair near an open volume of the Talmud that he had been studying.

Kanas could not understand nor explain such bestiality, why his fellow citizens eagerly volunteered to murder Jews and with such enthusiasm and relish – and extreme cruelty.

Was it the promise of taking possession of their homes and material assets or the anti-Semitic education they received at school or at home or in the church coupled with the propaganda that came off the Nazi printing press and on the radio?

"Probably both", Kanas muttered to himself.

Kanas himself had heard a prominent theologian on a popular radio program say,

"The Jews were responsible for both world wars. It is logical therefore that Jews should be exterminated."

Just the preceding day he had read a publication that left not an iota of doubt about the future of the Jews in Lithuania:

'...you must inform the Jews that their fate has been sealed....there must be such an anti-Jewish climate in the country that not a single Jew would even dare imagine that

Jews would have any minimal rights... Jews, your history in Lithuanian land that has lasted for 500 years is now over. Have no hopeful illusions!'

"Yes," he said to himself, "there were Jews who welcomed the Soviet occupation of Lithuania in 1940, which amongst other things resulted in the exile and murder of many Lithuanians, Jews included. But so did many others rejoice when the Soviets took over."

He knew though that when Nazi Germany took over his beloved country from Soviet control, in less than a week at the end of June 1941, things would never ever be the same. He would never have been able to imagine that before the year's end, more than 80% of Lithuanian's Jews (including close friends, colleagues and acquaintances) would be exterminated.

By 1944, more than 95% of all Lithuanian's Jews would be murdered – possibly the greatest percentage in all of Europe; and that the rate of collaboration amongst the Lithuanian community – amongst the highest in Europe, enabled all this to happen.

What is especially painful for him as he sits in his office is the knowledge that there is no one defending the basic rights of his Jewish neighbors, colleagues and friends.

A World of Pains, Solly Kaplinski, 2015

And while he takes on a variety of cases from couples confronting divorce to those accused of white-collar crimes like theft and corruption, and also represents some clients in murder trials, Kanas cannot reconcile his practice and knowledge of the law with the realities of life on the very streets where his office is located. He is bitterly disillusioned.

He knows too that there is very little he can do to stand up to this blatant injustice and in his eyes, a total breakdown of law and order, where one's basic human rights were being trampled on. He is in mourning for his beloved country where criminal practice and deviant behavior have now become the norm.

To all intents and purposes, he is a bystander and in his determination, he is as guilty as the perpetrators of these crimes. He feels that he is an enabler to what is going on all around him. He has nowhere to hide – and has no excuse except for his overriding and paralyzing fear. "I am a coward," he says to himself bitterly.

As trust slowly builds up between Kanas and Yonas, he begins to share his feelings with and confide his innermost thoughts to Yonas.

"It pains me what is happening in our country. Yes, I am continuing to defend my clients with integrity and I will fight for them to have their day in court. But Yonas, see with your own eyes what's happening here on our own street, on Stefanska."

"Mr. Kanas, I don't want to get involved in politics. I am very happy and feel privileged to be working for you. And I know from our very first meeting how you feel about the Jews. I have tried to avoid getting into discussions and debates with you about them.

I am torn – between the loyalties I have to my country, to you who I have grown to respect deeply, and to what I know to be true about Jews. Bottom line: they have their own religion and practices, they keep to themselves, they don't care about the other people around them who are not Jewish, and they don't share their wealth with their neighbors – only with their own kind.

So why should I be concerned about them? Why should I worry about them? Yes, I did know some Jews from school and in my neighborhood. And yes, some of them were reasonably decent people but overall, I don't owe them a thing. And I truly believe that our country will be better off without them."

"But Yonas, try to imagine for a moment that they are just ordinary and simple people like you and me.

A World of Pains, Solly Kaplinski, 2015

Forget about the word, 'Jewish.' All they want to do is to feed their families, educate their children, make love to their wives, earn a decent living and simply get on with their lives.

You have worked with me now for more than a year. You see how I try to protect and defend my clients.

You have also seen how many of them were ultimately found innocent thanks to my defense of them and your assistance that I have begun to value and appreciate.

Doesn't it bother you even just a little that there is a group of people just outside this office, on our doorstep who have no protection whatsoever?"

"Mr. Kanas, even if it did upset me – and I am not pretending to be blind to what's going on, but even if I wanted to help, what could I do?

Besides, you know as well as I do, that anyone caught helping Jews puts his own life and the lives of his family at risk.

Why should I take such a chance? Why should I stick my neck out?

What's in it for me?"

The Varnas home, New Jersey: June 8, 1996

Sandra and Jonathan have just returned home in the late afternoon following a visit to the cemetery. It is the *Yortzeit*, of Sandra's mother – the twentieth anniversary of the day on which her mother, Sima, passed away.

As always on these memorial days, Sandra is weepy and fragile. Jonathan who was especially close to Sima also finds it difficult to contain himself.

As is the tradition in the Varnas household, a small group of family and friends are invited on these annual days of remembrance to their home to quietly reflect on and celebrate the life of Sima.

Normally on these occasions, the people who are present drink a toast to Sima's memory, eat a few snacks, engage in small talk and then make their way home. This being the twentieth anniversary of Sima's passing, Sandra feels that this is a special milestone worthy of a few words from her.

"Sima, my dearly beloved mother of blessed memory", Sandra begins, "was a down to earth, uncomplicated lady who enjoyed the simple things in life. A sweet soul, Sima held the family together in the most trying and difficult of

A World of Pains, Solly Kaplinski, 2015

circumstances. She was always so generous in her praise of others and with a capacity for contentment with her lot in life not given to many.

I will not dwell on our past – the memory of the Shoah years and the degradation she suffered is too painful to contemplate but suffice to say that when we came to America, all that my mother could think of was my wellbeing. She dedicated herself totally to my welfare and put me first at all times.

A promising concert pianist before the war, she was destined for a glorious career as a musician. Her late mother was a Professor of Music at the Jewish Music Institute in Vilnius. However, here in America, my mother made a decision that her only child – me, was the center of her universe.

My mother lived for and through me. Nothing else mattered and sadly, she never played the piano again - except on one occasion when she sat at the piano in our home next to Ruben who was six years old at the time. He was learning to play the piano and was painstakingly trying to string some notes together. It sounded like Chopsticks!"

There was an audible although somewhat muted giggle in the room.

"He asked my mother to show him how to play the piano. Could she say no to her grandchild with his beautiful, pleading eyes? She tickled the ivories for a few moments – perhaps for the first time in almost forty years and voila, within seconds, the majestic beauty of Frederic Chopin was wafting through our home as if the master himself was seated at our piano! Mommy, you sacrificed your life totally for me! All that talent and creativity lost forever.

I can still hear her saying, 'All I want is a tranquil existence and happiness for my daughter. Is it too much to ask for, too much to expect?'

Mommy used to say to all her friends with pride: 'I have no riches, no possessions, and no wealth at all. But Sandrineleh is my jewel, my shining diamond, my precious possession!'

The fact that I stand before you today as Mrs. Jonathan Varnas, wife of my soul mate Jonathan, whom I treasure so very much, mother of two wonderful sons, a Judge of the New York Supreme Court is almost totally due to her selflessness and dedication – and her unconditional love.

I also want with your permission to take a moment to remember my father, my daddy, who was taken from me, from us so violently.

I can still hear the lilting lullabies you used to sing to me, the soft touch of your hand holding mine, your warm and loving kiss on my cheek.

Tateleh, daddy, all… all that remains …is a permanent scar on the heart."

Sandra takes out a Kleenex to wipe away the tears.

"*Mameleh*, my mommy, I was always in awe of your indomitable spirit and your strength of character and how you rose above those harsh, painful and humiliating experiences that were sent your way.

Perhaps the greatest lesson you taught me is that when all is said and done, how we are ultimately judged is not whether we put our minds in the way of great things but rather our concern for 'everydayness' and how we managed the mundane; not whether we 'did it in style' but whether we were unheroic and 'inconspicuously pious'.

Mommy, what especially stays with me after all these years and I thank you so much for this insight is that in the final analysis, the finished portrait of ourselves should be admired not for its painstakingly hewed frame however beautifully and exquisitely adorned, but for the concern, sense of loyalty and fair play we enacted on behalf of others.

I raise my glass to you and to your memory, I kiss you and I thank you and think of you as always with tears in my heart."

Jonathan asks his partner, Gene, to stay for dinner and later, over drinks that they enjoy together in Jonathan's study, Gene, normally jovial and extroverted, is in a mellow, somber mood.

"Ok, Gene, out with it. Something is clearly bothering you. What's going on?"

"Jonathan, I was so overcome by Sandra's words today, in fact, I was moved to tears. Something Sandra said about Sima triggered thoughts about my late father. I never had a warm relationship with him - always found him somewhat distant. His head was constantly buried in a book or an article about the Holocaust. It was almost an obsession. He could in the blink of an eye recite facts and dates – and actual days of specific events during the Shoah – like a robot, but expression of feelings, emotions - no.

He too like Sima would've been destined for a great career: a graduate of the University of Paris medical school, ground breaking published research, a life so full of promise and potential - and then a Jew on the run, a partisan in the forests, a concentration camp inmate - and forever fucked up afterwards.

Unable to work as a doctor after the war and always battling to make ends meet, he was haunted permanently by nightmares and screams and pain filled recurring dreams - and a trail of poverty, failure and mediocrity.

I don't think a night passed by without me hearing his screams and cries.

A World of Pains, Solly Kaplinski, 2015

Unz tragt und Gott lagt- we plot and we make all sorts of plans but all the while, God is laughing. He has other ideas for us. We would like to think that we are the masters of our own destiny that we can plan our own fate, but in the real world, one's dreams, ambitions and aspirations are often thwarted and go up in smoke. My father no longer had his good name, his reputation and his self-respect. He lost his profession – and himself.

What gave him some fulfillment in his later years was being called on to give evidence in a trial of two Nazi officers in Mainz, Germany who were accused of the murder of hundreds of Jews. And Jonathan, if there's one thing I will forever remember and respect him for it is his stirring words at the trial which always echo somewhere in the background for me:

'I feel that I am the messenger of a group that has been annihilated. I am their representative. I have to do my duty to the dead and for the dead. They, the victims, cannot speak, but their souls seem to be drifting through the chambers demanding justice and I will speak on their behalf.

The memories of
my parents, brothers and sisters
of teachers, friends and comrades

the ear piercing sounds of children in tears as they are being led to the slaughter

make it so difficult for me to convey in words what I am feeling and the agony I am enduring as I observe the two accused sitting under heavy guard, shuffling papers and documents noisily, frequently scowling at the audience and the witnesses.'

The image of my father in so much pain, but calling for justice and not revenge - even as the accused gave the SS salute and shouted in a bellicose way, *Heil Hitler!* I think probably influenced me more than anything or anyone else to take up the law profession."

Gene stands up to pour himself another scotch. Jonathan is sitting engrossed He wants to interject. There are so many questions he would like to ask but decides that for him to interrupt now would stop the flow of Gene's personal outpourings, which is a rare occasion.

Gene sits down again, is quiet for a few moments and then continues.

"My father was also in demand as a speaker in the community and while he rarely spoke about his own personal and emotional experiences preferring to dwell on the historical aspects of the Shoah, he clearly had a huge impact on his audiences.

The tributes that poured in after his death revealed another side of him that as a young boy growing up, I regrettably never saw nor appreciated.

I carry some of them perpetually in my wallet."

Gene takes his wallet out of his back pocket and opens it to retrieve some of the tributes.

"Jonathan, let me read you just a few:

'Your father was a symbol of courage and determination in the face of overwhelming odds.'

'Despite all the physical and mental persecution, which he endured, he nevertheless showed great courage and fortitude in the face of those tremendous hardships.'

'After hearing him speak on the Shoah when I was in high school, to me, he was a man who had a tremendous amount of feeling and sympathy for his fellow beings. It is men like your father who give us youngsters hope for the future.'

'His contribution was the inspiration of a special spark in his soul.'

'May you find comfort in the expression of affection and esteem by those who knew him.'

'You can be proud of the honor, which your father bestowed upon the community.'

But in bitter truth, my father, as a Holocaust survivor, seemed at times to be living on a different planet. And when he died several years ago, suddenly and unexpectedly, we never really reconciled.

I didn't have the chance to say good-bye, to mend any broken fences, to resolve any outstanding conflicts, to have closure. Not that there was bad blood between us, but there was little warmth and I know that I never really tried to make the effort to understand his tortured and tormented soul.

Perhaps too immature. Maybe too busy working my butt off to consider anyone else. Too damn selfish....or probably... too scared to pry open the past.

If only I had been a better son, more considerate of his needs, kinder, softer – especially given his trials and tribulations.

I guess these "if only's" will stay with me for the rest of my days, a perpetual shame. All the repentances on Yom Kippur, the Day of Atonement, all the remembrances on his *Yortzeit*, the yearly anniversary of his death, all the lighting of candles to honor his memory, all the recitings of the *Kaddish*, the mourner's prayer, will not assuage the feelings of guilt that cling to me leech like and will not let go.

Sandra somehow in her few words of tribute today conveyed so much about her very close relationship with Sima and her appreciation for her sacrifices. I know my dad worked incredibly hard and took on several jobs to enable me to go to school and complete my university studies but I never really thanked him or showed my appreciation. I always took it for granted and you can't imagine how I feel."

Gene brushes away tears from his eyes with his hand and stares into the distance.

"Gene, this is the first time since we have known each other that you have opened up about your father. Despite our long friendship, I noticed that you always avoided talking about your parents – and your father in particular. It's obviously very painful for you to talk about this and of course, I don't judge you in any way for not sharing this with me. If you feel comfortable perhaps you would like to tell me more about him?"

"I will only tell you the following and then I'm closing this door. I've had enough of carrying this debilitating burden of the Shoah on my shoulders, of living in its long shadow. I want to draw a line under it. I want to press 'delete!' It weighs me down at times and messes with my mind and my emotions. If I should ever, God forbid, suffer from Alzheimer's, will the Shoah be the only thing that I remember?"

Gene drains the last drops of whiskey from his glass, sits back in his chair and closes his eyes, seemingly falling asleep.

Jonathan sits in silence contemplating Gene's pain as a child of Holocaust survivors and marveling at the fact that it has been so well camouflaged - until now.

"My father," Gene continues after what seems like an eternity, "was in the Plazow Nazi concentration camp in a German occupied area of Poland. Amon Goeth was the camp commander. He was an especially sadistic and brutal beast. You may remember him from the Schindler's List movie. For pleasure, he used to stand on his balcony and shoot at and murder people on the grounds below him. People were terrified whenever he was around. Shit scared and shit scarred - that was my father.

He only opened up to me once and never again about how he

A World of Pains, Solly Kaplinski, 2015

as a young boy, on Yom Kippur in 1943 together with 15 000 inmates were assembled on the ground in front of Goeth's balcony. They were forced to witness how Goeth and his SS-men took fifty Jews from the barracks and then shot them in cold blood, as if engaged in sport. Some prisoners in addition were publically hanged.

The image that stayed with my father forever – and with me as with all those terrified people assembled on the ground, was how a young boy of about fourteen, Haubenstock was his name, was about to be hanged on Goeth's orders. It was said in the camp that young Haubenstock had sung a Russian tune. A rope was slung around the boy's neck, a high chair was removed and unbelievably, the rope snapped.

The boy was again lifted on to a high chair that was placed under the rope, and he began to beg for mercy. An order was given to hang him a second time. And then he was raised a second time to the gallows, and hanged, and thereafter that same piece of dreck, Amon Goeth, fired a shot point blank at the still dangling body. *Farwus*.....why?

That's the only thing my father ever mentioned about his experiences during the Holocaust. And yet...so many things left unsaid, unexplained, unexpressed and unshared.

I couldn't even get a foot in the door.

Jonathan, tell me how I could empathize with the trauma of his tragic life experience if to all intents and purposes, he kept me in the dark, he shut me out?

In some ways, I don't blame him. Perhaps it was just too painful for him to open up. Maybe he was determined to protect me from the evils in the world, to wrap me in cotton wool – but in reality, there was a sense of denial in our home and I… we… lived a lie.

And that's all I will ever say on this subject. He always remained a fucked up victim – and so do I."

Soon after Gene left, Jonathan went up to the bedroom hoping to talk with Sandra about Sima – and about what had transpired with Gene but she was already sleeping after a stress-filled day.

Jonathan took a long shower and tried to sleep but kept on tossing and turning, the image of the murdered boy swaying on the rope a constant presence.

Eventually several hours later, he fell into a deep but troubled sleep.

Sandra wakes up to hear Jonathan shrieking in his sleep,

"No. It can't be. It's not me. I didn't do it. I didn't do it."

Sandra reaches out to hold him and wakes him up.

A World of Pains, Solly Kaplinski, 2015

"Jonathan, you're having a horrible nightmare. Please tell me what's going on?"

Jonathan tries to catch his breath. He is agitated and shivering and his mouth is dry. Sandra drapes a blanket around him and gives him some water. She hugs him tight. He is gripped with terror. A few minutes pass before he is able to speak. "Sandra, I can't remember all of it but it's horrifying. I saw a... a young infant thrown violently into the air and somehow... I...I think I am involved and connected to this child in some way, that perhaps I know the little baby. I don't know how to explain this but I...I may be part of this horrific story. I had a similar type of – call it a vision, a few months ago. As I was shaving, out of the blue, I saw an image in the mirror of an infant...being thrown into the air."

"Jonathan, it's probably connected to the traumatic Wolfman case. It's just too much of a coincidence for it not to be. I know how deeply involved you have been with the case and how caught up you are – which is always so typical of you. You throw yourself into your cases body and soul – and become totally dedicated to them and to your clients.

I know you are stressed. Let me comfort you my love, my precious. You are my life. You belong to me." She kisses him tenderly on the lips and slowly unbuttons his pajamas.

In the morning on the way to work, Jonathan wonders whether Gene relating his father's story in Plazow has somehow shaped his dream or perhaps Sandra is right: it is the Wolfman case that is constantly preying on his mind and is preoccupying him somehow affecting his dreams.

He decides to make an appointment with Dr. Max Bromberg, one of the top psychiatrists in the city who is known for amongst other things his expertise in dream interpretation.

Jonathan does not mention this to Sandra.

Kanas and Yonas: January, 1944

Yonas notices that Kanas barely leaves the office.

He also seems to be more preoccupied than usual with matters unrelated to his work and appears to be under considerable stress with beads of perspiration on his forehead even on the coldest of days.

Kanas barely touches his food over shared lunches with Yonas.

He tells Yonas one day that he will no longer accept new clients. Yonas is shocked since in the few years he has been with Kanas, he never saw him turn anyone away.

A World of Pains, Solly Kaplinski, 2015

A few weeks later, Kanas tells Yonas that he has to leave Vilnius immediately – in fact that night, to visit his family in the countryside and that he does not know how long he will be away.

"Does that mean I no longer have work with you Mr. Kanas?"

"I suggest that you enquire whether there are other jobs available, Yonas. I have seen how you have grown and matured over the last two years working with me. Of course I will give you outstanding references."

"Obviously I am deeply disappointed that you are leaving. It has been a great honor to be your assistant. I have learned so much from you.

I also need to tell you that this has been my second home. You have been very much of a father figure for me and while I know there have been times that we have disagreed - especially when it comes to the Jews, please know that I admire you tremendously and will be forever grateful to you for taking a chance on me."

"I appreciate your kind words, Yonas. Perhaps one day we will reunite when the situation in our country has changed. I predict a great future for you and I am pleased to have played a small part in influencing the tracks of your life."

They shake hands and hug each other and Yonas leaves Kanas's office rather dejectedly.

Several hours later, he remembers that he has a spare set of keys to the office at his apartment. Despite the lateness of the hour – around 11.00 pm, he makes his way back to the office to return them.

As he approaches the office, he notices that Kanas's rooms are in darkness, which is unusual since for security reasons, Kanas always leaves a light on in his office.

Yonas also sees a car parked outside the office. The engine is running but there is no one inside.

He runs up the flight of stairs, turns the key in the lock, opens the door and hears the crashing of something or someone falling to the floor.

Yonas is bewildered; he does not know what is happening. He feels scared. His pulse is racing. Perhaps Kanas's office is being burgled? Yonas's heart pounds fast.

"Yonas, is that you?"

"Mr. Kanas, what's happening? Is everything okay?"

There is a stunned silence and then the beam of a flashlight. Yonas makes out a face in the dark which he doesn't recognize and then another –someone crouching on the floor.

"Mr. Kanas, what's going on? I... I don't understand?"

A World of Pains, Solly Kaplinski, 2015

"Yonas, I don't have a choice now but to trust to you and to hope that you will do the right thing. This is the wife and daughter of my former partner, Jacob Rothstein, who was forcibly removed from his office two years ago and has not been seen again. I saw with my own eyes how fellow Lithuanians dragged him out by his hair, cursing him, pummeling him with rubber truncheons and their bloodied fists and screaming that the time had come 'for the zhid, the fucking Jew, to pay for his sins!'

I have hidden Mrs. Rothstein and Sandrina in my office basement ever since. It is now getting too dangerous – the authorities have become suspicious and are searching for Jews everywhere.

I am taking them with me to my family who have a farm in the country. Will you join me – or turn us in?

You need to make a decision immediately."

On a farm near Vilnius: March, 1944

Sandrina and her mother, Simonas, despite the ever-present dangers, felt safe and secure on the farm knowing that Kanas was looking after them. He had been a family friend for many years and together with Jacob Rothstein, his law partner for more than thirty years, they built up a successful legal practice.

Kanas, being a bachelor, had often eaten at their home and was regarded as one of the family and trustworthy.

The farm belonged to Kanas's brother, Karolis, and provided a safe haven for Sandrina and Simonas.

Karolis like his brother Kanas was extremely hard working and while he had in the past been a successful fruit and vegetable farmer, the farm was now in a neglected and run down state because of the war. Karolis and his family could barely subsist on whatever vegetables and fruit they were still able to grow. They survived mainly on a diet of boiled potatoes, insects, and whatever edible plants and small animals they were able to find.

Yonas was happy to become a farm hand and help with whatever chores were required. He also stood guard and kept

A World of Pains, Solly Kaplinski, 2015

a lookout for unexpected visitors - Nazi soldiers who were searching for Jews or Lithuanian collaborators who were happy to turn in their fellow citizens to be murdered for harboring Jews - and then claim their rewards.

The farm was situated on the edge of the forest and in preparation for the regular search missions for Jews, Yonas built a small, modest bunker underground using a long unused exterior basement that provided adequate protection from the killer squads – and from prying neighbors.

As an added measure of safety and security, Sandrina and Simonas spent most days hidden in the bunker sleeping on straw, with no running water, nor toilets, nor heat. Simonas, a woman of slender build, often slept on top of Sandrina to keep her warm. There were days that they had stay silent for several hours at a time.

While Karolis was able to provide some food, Sandrina and Simonas were often hungry and Yonas would go into the forest and forage for food – often unsuccessfully which necessitated eating boiled grass on a number of occasions.

One icy cold winter's day, German soldiers turned up very early in the morning and began an extensive search of the farm. Yonas managed to warn Sandrina and Simonas to stay in the bunkers and not utter a sound.

After a comprehensive but unsuccessful search, the commandant of the soldiers began interrogating Yonas demanding to know where the Jews were hidden on the farm.

"I know", said Commandant Schuler "that there are Jews hiding here. The neighboring farmer told me. Where are they?" he shouted, cocking his rifle.

"Believe me", said Yonas, "if they were here, I would hand them over to you immediately. Firstly, I can't stand them – they are vermin and bloodsuckers. Secondly, with war rations and our hunger here, do you think I would share our meager food reserves with anyone, but especially Jews?

And do you think I wouldn't want to claim the rewards that have been offered?"

The commandant beckons to Yonas to come closer and pretends to whisper in his ear. Without warning, he slams his fist with full force into Yonas's face. He falls to the ground, his face dripping with blood.

"In case you have any second thoughts about wanting to help Rosenshayn and Lindenstein and Blumenfeld and Katz and Hirsch or Strauss …those *kackfass yids*….there's more where this came from.

And if you have any doubts, *schweinhund*, pull down their trousers and look at their *schwanz*."

During the course of the many months on the farm, Yonas and Sandrina, who was a few years younger than he was, barely exchanged a word. That all changed when Kanas became extremely ill and needed around the clock care and supervision. Simonas, Sandrina, Karolis and Yonas took turns to stay at his side and to tend to all his needs.

Kanas's illness brought them all closer together as they tried both singly and together to nurse him back to health.

One evening, when it was Yonas's turn to look after him, Kanas in a strained whisper turned to him and said:

"Yonas, I don't know how much longer I have to live. I feel weak and have no energy. I have grown to love you as my own son and I am concerned what may happen to you in the future.

When this war ends and it will end, Lithuania will not be a safe place to live in. You need to make your way to America. I have asked my brother to arrange fake documents for you that will give you a new name and identity - and a new profession – a lawyer.

I want you to re-invent yourself. Become someone else. That will be the only way to survive.

The Jews talk about America being *der goldene medina* – the country of gold, a land of opportunity. Go and make your name, fame and fortune there. You have all the attributes to make a tremendous success of your life. Moreover, I am charging you with the responsibility of looking after Simonas and Sandrine. They have no one left in this goddam awful world but you."

Ellis Island: May, 1946

Yonas was overwhelmed when he saw the Statue of Liberty as his boat sailed into Ellis Island.

He had never seen anything as beautiful and uplifting as Liberty, the figure of a woman with broken shackles at her feet who is poised with her golden torch to bring freedom and enlightenment to the human race.

He felt that he had reached the land of promise and opportunity.

He showed his identity papers to the Immigration Inspector who stamped his documents after a cursory glance, and he waited for Simonas and Sandrina to have their applications processed.

A World of Pains, Solly Kaplinski, 2015

The Ellis Island experience proved to be harsh initially with people in uniforms pointing fingers and issuing commands in a language that fearful immigrants could not understand. And then there were the doctors who in a brief examination searching for diseases or disabilities that could possibly exclude would - be immigrants, hurried about dedicating less than two minutes to each immigrant.

Fortunately, Simonas, Sandrine and Yonas, now Sima, Sandra and Jonathan, were able to negotiate all the hurdles of Ellis Island with relative ease. They were able to persuade the officials that with their professions as a lawyer (although Jonathan would need to take some courses to qualify to practice in America) and professor of music, they would not be a burden on the State; they would not be a public charge.

The fact that Sima had a brother who was waiting to meet them and who guaranteed a roof over their heads on the Lower East Side also helped pave the way.

During the preceding year, but especially on the boat coming to America, Sima, Sandra and Jonathan became especially close with each other – almost like family.

On the journey where they were packed in like sardines, they only had each other to turn to and comfort, to put the past behind them, to plan for the future.

It was inevitable that in a new country, with a strange language and a different culture, the ease of immigration would depend on finding a place to live, getting jobs but more important, having people that one could trust and confide in.

The bonds formed among Sima, Sandra and Jonathan grew stronger with each passing day and while it was never discussed or even intimated, it became clear to Sima that the developing friendship between Sandra and Jonathan was growing and she silently approved.

Jonathan had proved to be a tower of strength on the farm and on their long journey to America – and had saved their lives at considerable risk to himself.

He was also ambitious to get ahead, would prove in Sima's estimation to be an excellent provider, was respectful and deferential to both of them and seemed to be a person of strong values.

What more could she ask for her daughter?

A World of Pains, Solly Kaplinski, 2015

Doctor Max Bromberg's office: July 10, 1996

Jonathan is shown into Dr. Bromberg's office and sits down in an easy chair directly opposite Max. They shake hands. An oak coffee table on which stand a pitcher of water, several glasses and a bowl of candies, separates them. There is also a couch in one corner of the room.

The office has the usual book- lined floor to ceiling stacks and features prominently photographs of Max and what seems to be his family - his attractive wife and three daughters, happily posing at the seaside with the family dog.

"Firstly, Jonathan, people who have toiled in the field of human rights and have championed the underdog have always inspired me so to meet one of America's major proponents is a special privilege. And congratulations by the way for winning the Presidential Medal of Freedom.

Now I know that this is not what you have come here to discuss. What I'd like to ask you is if you can tell me why you are here, what concerns you, and if you can sketch a brief personal history."

"Thanks, Max, if I can call you Max, for your kind sentiments. I assume that whatever I say to you is in confidence. This is the first time I am giving anyone this potted history. Whenever I have been asked in the past about myself, I have always indicated that I am a product of the tragedy of the war- torn years in Europe and that it's too painful a topic for me to talk about.

Please forgive me for being brief.

Since you mentioned my involvement in human rights, I think I can perhaps tie that into my family history. I was a Second World War victim who personally saw Jews being killed on the streets of Vilnius.

A lawyer for whom I worked and who had a profound influence on my life was hiding a young Jewish child and her mother in the basement of his office.

He decided to escape with them to the countryside to his cousin's farm where they were hidden for more than two years – at great risk.

I accompanied them and was involved in helping them hide from the Nazis and their collaborators.

I lost touch with my own parents and siblings who I believe were killed at the front.

We were constantly on the run for a few years, living in the most extreme of conditions especially during the intense winters but the will and the motivation to survive were great.

After the war, I managed to make my way to America together with the mother and daughter. I subsequently married Sandra, the daughter, who is now a judge of the New York Supreme Court; we have two sons who are studying at Oxford.

Sandra is my friend, my anchor and my life and my feelings for her grow stronger with the passage of time. She has given me the space to grow, to accomplish and to succeed in almost everything I do. I love her with all my heart and soul.

It pains me so deeply that I can't share our session with her yet and believe me, I am conflicted on this. On the one hand, Sandra sees me as someone who is an achiever and highly successful. On the other hand, if she knows I am in therapy, she may see it as a failure for me and I don't want to give her any pause to doubt me. We have been through too much together and I need to be strong for her. I also need her to be strong for me.

It is also to be honest Max – and please don't take this personally, a *shandeh*, an embarrassment for me to consult with a psychiatrist, to have to lean on you for help.

I have always prided myself on being independent, being able to stand on my own two feet and not having to look over my shoulder. I am deeply respected by my peers, colleagues and friends for my work as a lawyer and as an advocate for human rights. And I have won numerous awards for my accomplishments.

How would it look in public for Jonathan Varnas, the big shot *macher*, a VIP who makes things happen, to be consulting a psychiatrist?

I know this sounds confusing Max but I would appreciate it if in the meantime, we kept these sessions confidential from my wife."

Max nods his head in agreement but makes a mental note to follow up later. This doesn't sound right.

He is also tempted to ask Jonathan why, if he has all these misgivings about seeing a psychiatrist, he is actually sitting opposite him – but decides to let it go.

"With regard to my work, I have been a partner in my law firm which I co-founded, for almost forty years.

In addition to my work as a lawyer, my partners have been generous enough to allow me the time to get involved in the field of human rights. I have been blessed to be able to play a small part in helping to improve the lives of disadvantaged people especially children and giving them some dignity and hope for the future.

I believe by the way that my war experience is one of the

reasons I am involved in this endeavor. In a sense, I am trying to complete the gestalt of a broken family and make up for the loss of my family by being of service to others, helping to rehabilitate fractured families and damaged children.

In my legal capacity, my practice has been rather eclectic. I have represented my clients in a variety of fields from fraud, to victims of child abuse to murder. I am currently involved in the Wolfman case that I am sure you have been aware of from its constant high profile exposure in the media. You can't escape it!"

"I haven't really been following the case too closely. Tell me briefly about it?"

Jonathan reaches out for the pitcher and pours himself some water. He offers Max, who with a wave of the finger indicates that he doesn't want any. "Wolfman has been accused of the murder of his son (unless paternity tests prove otherwise) in the most horrific of circumstances. He has confessed to what he did, is deeply remorseful and wants to pay the price for his crime. I am his defense lawyer and will be trying to establish mitigating circumstances that will allow for a reduced sentence. What has impressed and moved me, Max, is his acknowledgement of his guilt and his strong need to be held accountable. You rarely find this amongst felons."

"So why are you here, Jonathan?"

"I don't know if it's stress I am going through as a result of the case but lately, I have not been sleeping well and have also experienced – I don't know how best to describe it - the recurrence of two images that have left me feeling anxious."

"Tell me about these images."

Jonathan pours some more water into his glass. He takes a few sips. Max notices that there is a marked tremor in Jonathan's hand. The glass falls from his fingers, shattering into many tiny pieces on the parquet floor and all over the shaggy carpet. "Don't worry about this Jonathan. I will sort it out later. Please go on."

"Once while I was shaving, I thought I saw behind me in the mirror the rough outline of what looked like an infant in the air. It was just a split second image.

The other night, maybe in a dream, I saw the image again but this time more clearly: the body was fuller, the face features more sharply defined and while I didn't recognize the face itself, there was something about the image and the situation that gave me some sense of familiarity. That's all I can remember at this stage.

Had it been a one off occurrence, I would have ignored it. I have to say that now, having experienced an almost identical situation, I have cause for some concern. I am baffled as to what this may mean and to be honest, a little fearful. This is worrying me and that is why I am here."

"Jonathan, I want you to close your eyes, take a few deep breaths …and relax for a few moments."

Other than the ticking of the clock and Jonathan's breathing, there is silence in the office.

"Jonathan, is there anything else you want to tell me?"

A few minutes pass. The silence continues. Jonathan slowly opens his eyes and looks at Max – with a blank stare. He doesn't say a word.

"I think we will stop at this point – until next week same time. I want to also give you a prescription for low dosage valium that will help you relax. One a day should be enough."

Max is relieved that the session has ended. He felt for a moment that the process was moving too quickly. He knows that for communication between them not to be shut down and more important for trust to develop, Jonathan needs to proceed slowly to unpack the issues that concern him and that more than anything else, he needs to feel safe.

Yad Vashem, Jerusalem: June 22, 1996

"To sum up," says the Chair of the panel, a retired Justice of the Israel Supreme Court, "we have debated this case for several days and I would like to argue to my respected and deeply esteemed commission members why I think he is worthy of being awarded the title of Righteous among the Nations:

He meets all our criteria:

He saved Jews from the threat of death – in the face of extreme danger to himself.

He therefore put his own life at risk by defying the authorities and the prevailing norms against Jews.

He did not ask, demand nor receive any financial recompense for his brave deeds.

We have checked and rechecked the testimony and documentation of those who are applying for this great honor on his behalf. It all adds up beyond a measure of doubt.

I think he would be a worthy recipient of this prestigious award."

A World of Pains, Solly Kaplinski, 2015

Miriam, one of the commissioners who is a retired school principal and herself a survivor is deep in thought. The words of Eli Wiesel whom she so admires, ring in her ears:

"While not all victims were Jews, all Jews were victims."

For her, Yad Vashem, a memorial to commemorate, document, research, and educate about the Holocaust, is almost like a second home.

She has been involved with Yad Vashem in various capacities - primarily as an educator and a witness, since its inception more than forty years ago.

Both her parents and brother perished in Auschwitz and she never married.

The Righteous among the Nations, a small, elite and courageous group of people, are for Miriam the one shining light in a time of extreme darkness for the Jewish people.

"Well my dear colleagues, we have spent hours of deliberations. It is time to make the decision..."

Doctor Max Bromberg's office: September 1, 1996

"Jonathan, this is our sixth session together. We, or rather you, have spoken about what you remember from your early childhood, the influence of your parents – good and bad, your school days, and the impact that Kanas has had on your life.

I have just been a listener at this stage.

You have also spoken about your ongoing, to quote you, 'love affair' with your wife, Sandra, as well as how proud you both are of your sons.

I have a feeling though that we are not getting any nearer to understanding the images that you saw.

We have been skirting around this. I have been holding off on this for quite a while since I didn't want you to feel pressurized. I want you to move at your own pace and level of comfort. But what I am slowly beginning to understand is and I think you alluded to this earlier, that there may be a connection however tenuous, between the Wolfman case and the images that have given you cause for concern.

Let's try to understand what's happening with you. Let's explore this together."

A World of Pains, Solly Kaplinski, 2015

"Max, I've also been wondering whether such a link exists but I am struggling to make a connection. Maybe it's the stress of this particular case, all the hype it has been getting but for heaven's sake, what do the images have to do with it?"

"Jonathan, I think what we have to try and establish is what's driving the images since I believe that they are symptoms of the underlying problems.

Perhaps you can tell me what bothers you the most about the Wolfman case. What's the one thing that really stands out for you, that makes you upset or perhaps even torments you?"

"What Stevie did with his child - violently throwing a helpless defenseless infant out of the car and killing him is something that stays with me all the time. I have been unable to get rid of this picture. It just haunts and horrifies me."

"I don't blame you for how you feel. It is not only a despicable and shocking act; it goes against the grain of all normal civilized human behavior. We, I think, all feel as agitated as you do."

"Yes, but why can't I let it go? I have always prided myself on not letting my emotions cloud my professional judgment. I have, at all times that I can think of in my professional career, been able to stand back, to compartmentalize myself, to differentiate between my role as a lawyer and any personal feelings I may have about my cases and about the clients I am serving. Sometimes as a result, I seem to be aloof and give the impression of being unsympathetic and not showing any empathy which is far from the truth. I care about my clients very much but as a rule, I favor the cerebral, clinical approach. In this case however, I have been unable to make the distinction. I am consumed by this emotionally. I have nothing but deep-seated anger towards Wolfman and what he did.

I have in fact been thinking of possibly recusing myself from the case.

My emotional state and my personal feelings are clearly affecting the high professional standards I have set for myself."

"Jonathan, put that possibility on hold for the moment. Let's stop at this point and pick this up again next week."

That night, Amon Goeth appears vividly in Jonathan's dream hurling a baby child into the air and shooting at the child several times – like a hunter shooting at quail.

He is staring at Jonathan intensely, has a huge grin on his face and is flashing a V sign.

A World of Pains, Solly Kaplinski, 2015

The Varnas home: September, 1996

"Jonathan, there's a registered letter for you," says Sandra as he enters the house. He puts his bag down and picks up the envelope that has an Israeli postmark on it.

Jonathan has been to Israel several times in both his personal capacity with Sandra and the boys and as a member of various human rights delegations investigating claims of alleged abuses by Israeli soldiers in the disputed territories.

He has always felt uncomfortable in this latter capacity. In his opinion, not enough balance was shown with regard to abuse on the "other side" but in his zealousness for fair play and given that in his opinion, Israel, the stronger side, was holding most of the cards, he allowed his name to be attached to several reports critical of Israel. Given his status in the international community, this also added weight to the reports that were subsequently published.

Jonathan opened up the envelope and was surprised – pleasantly, to learn that Yad Vashem had given him the award of a Righteous among the Nations in recognition of his exceptional bravery in rescuing Jews.

"Sandra," he cried out, "I can't believe this. I didn't know anything about it. How were you able to keep the process a secret?"

"Well firstly congratulations and *mazel tov* my darling! This is so well - deserved and of course, I speak from firsthand experience!

This process has been going on for several years now, Jonathan. I didn't let you in on this since I didn't know whether this would be possible and I didn't want to raise your expectations.

My mother was working on this before she died, had written up everything you did to save us on the farm. I only got round to working on this a few years ago.

I am so happy for you. This wonderful news could not have come at a better time."

She hugs and kisses him tenderly on the lips.

"I'll go and prepare dinner Jonathan and I know what you will do!"

Sure enough, Jonathan goes to the liquor cabinet and opens up an 18 Years Old Glenmorangie that he has been saving for a special occasion.

He sits in his easy chair to savor the moment of this elite award. He raises his glass to a faded photograph of Kanas on the mantelpiece, the only one he has in his possession.

A World of Pains, Solly Kaplinski, 2015

"This one's for you Kanas. You made me. You transformed me. You were my mentor, my moral guide and my friend. You pointed me in the right direction.

I feel a bit of a fraud receiving this award. It should have been you. I wish I had met you earlier in my life.... If only you had been my father...."

He remembers his last visit to Yad Vashem at the height of the violent intifada years and in particular, a conversation he had with a cab driver, Avi, who was taking him back to his hotel in Tel Aviv following the Yom Hashoah Holocaust Memorial Day ceremony at Yad Vashem.

"My parents grew up in the old city of Jerusalem," Avi begins, "and my mother had recurring nightmares which haunted her almost daily. She remembers as a five-year-old child how her father who was a plumber, was called to fix a faulty drain on the roof of his neighbor's house, an Arab family who were on good terms with the cab driver's grandfather and his family.

The old city was and still is a very mixed neighborhood with Jews and Arabs living very close to each other.

My mother, the then 5-year-old child, remembers her father going into the neighbor's home, climbing up onto the roof – quite a height, perhaps the equivalent of a few stories.

He stands on the roof looking down, waving happily at her, and then suddenly, he falls to the ground, a look of shock and bewilderment on his face and a loud cry as he crashes to his death. It was obvious that he had been pushed.

My family is raised on this horrific story. At our family *Shabbat* dinner table every Friday night, we paused to remember my *Saba*, my grandfather and to recall what happened to him.

It becomes part of the lore, the weekly ritual in our household where the story is recounted repeatedly. We are a very close family and this story becomes an integral part of our family identity.

Fast forward to the Yom Kippur War in 1973. I was stationed in the Sinai desert looking after captured Egyptian prisoners of war. I am so tired and exhausted and try to focus on my responsibility to guard the soldiers and to make sure that no one attempts to escape.

I don't know if I am in a dream but I see a pair of hands pushing my grandfather over the roof and without hesitating, I pull the trigger on these defenseless prisoners and kill a number of them before being forcibly restrained by a few of my fellow soldiers."

Jonathan is unable to respond – he is shocked.

A World of Pains, Solly Kaplinski, 2015

When he regains his senses he asks, "What happened afterwards?"

"I was sentenced by a military tribunal to five years in jail. Apparently, 'psychological factors' were taken into consideration."

"And did you have any regrets?"

"Only that I didn't kill more of them."

Jonathan sits back in his chair, deep in thought. "Between Wolfman, Amon Goeth and Avi, I am surrounded by murderers", he says out aloud. "I wonder if there will be any more killers who will come into my life."

Jonathan is feeling dizzy and lightheaded. His heart is pounding. He gets up to pour himself another whiskey to try to steady himself. He inserts Vivaldi's Four Seasons into the record player. He swallows a valium, sits down and tries to relax, shuts his eyes and thinks again about the Righteous Award.

"Do I truly deserve this?" he asks himself. "I feel like an imposter." He is unable to sit still, constantly fidgeting.

He eventually drains the glass and feels himself slowly drifting off…He is sitting on a plane, leaving Israel returning to New York via London where he has to spend a few days on business. His head is buried in the New York Times.

His visit has been hectic and the daily death and destruction on the buses, in the streets and at the cafes have debilitated him.

He is certainly not seeking to engage his neighbor seated next to him. Small talk is the last thing he needs. He is exhausted and all he wants is time out, to switch off from engaging the world around him.

He suddenly hears his neighbor say in a heavily accented voice,

"Do you live in London?"

"No," Jonathan replied, "I live in New York."

Jonathan returns to the New York Times but his neighbor not taking the hint, persists,

"How much time did you spend in Israel?"

"Ten days."

Jonathan has been engaged in conversation and he needs to be polite.

"Do you live in Israel?" Jonathan asks.

"Yes, but I am going to London."

"On holiday or business?"

"Well', he replied, "I am the Headmaster of a high school for students from overseas in the North of the country and I am going to visit a various schools in London to recruit some

A World of Pains, Solly Kaplinski, 2015

students for the new year - but that's not my primary reason for going. By the way, my name is Yehudi." He extends his hand to Jonathan.

Yehudi has opened a door and wants Jonathan to enter.

Jonathan turns the handle, "So why are you going?"

"I work for an organization in Israel that supports victims of terror, helps their families cope, and provides all sorts of support services to them in their darkest hours of grief and tragedy. I am going to speak to several groups of people in London about the very important work that this organization is engaged in," he continues.

Choking on his words, Jonathan blurts out, "How …how are you connected to this organization?"

"Well, I don't want to say anything which may upset you," he begins rather hesitantly, almost apologetically, "but a few months ago, we were traveling by car around midnight to Haifa after a *Bar Mitzvah simcha*, a confirmation celebration in Jerusalem."

Jonathan braces himself - he can guess what is coming.

"There's a wall which separates Kalkilya, a Palestinian city in the West Bank, from the road. Somehow, two terrorists used a pneumatic device to cut through bars in a sewer tunnel under the eight-meter-high security wall built around the outskirts of Kalkilya. The wall was built as part of security arrangements for travelers on this specific road. The two terrorists managed to dig below the wall, get near to the road, opened fire on our car and Shlomit, my beloved seven year old daughter, was murdered."

Tears well up and Jonathan begins sobbing – uncontrollably.

"I'm sorry if I have spoilt your flight", Yehudi says putting his arm on Jonathan's shoulder.

"The...the last thing you need to... do", Jonathan responds, "is ....to apologize." He struggles to find the words to express his sorrow for Yehudi's great loss. He thinks of his own sons.

A few minutes pass by. Jonathan has regained his composure.

"I need a favor," he asks of Jonathan. "I have to give a speech about my personal story, about what happened, in English, not my first language as you can hear. I want you to read it over to check if it's okay." He takes out two crumpled sheets of paper from his jacket pocket and hands them to Jonathan.

Jonathan looks at the first page but it's all a blur. His tears smudge the words. He can't continue.

"Listen", he tells Yehudi returning the stained pages, "You don't need a text; you don't need words on a page. Just follow your heart. The words will come automatically."

A World of Pains, Solly Kaplinski, 2015

During the *shiva*, the seven-day mourning period, Yehudi tells him, that amongst those who attended were his Arab neighbors who live very near his village and know him and his family.

Yehudi tells Jonathan that they feel very uncomfortable and ashamed of what their fellow Arabs have done but they want to be in his home to offer their condolences and share in his family's grief and mourning.

And sometime later, at the end of the Ramadan month of fasting, reflection and sexual abstinence, Yehudi was invited to his Arab neighbor's village to celebrate the feast of *Eid ul-Fitr*.

"Did you go?" Jonathan asks him, knowing the answer.

"Of course," he replies, "I can't turn down my neighbor's hospitality."

Jonathan is rooted to his chair, the image of Shlomit, the dead little girl, transfixed in his mind.

The offices of Greenberg, Goodman and Varnas, Manhattan: September 15, 1996

Jonathan arrives at the office early to prepare for the weekly Wolfman update meeting.

He pours himself a cup of coffee and sits down at his desk to read the briefs that have been prepared for him.

He gets through the first two pages but he can't concentrate. He cleans his reading glasses, stares at the page but he is unable to make out the words. He grips the page tightly and tries to focus but to his horror, the words are jumping off the page creating blank white spaces, and pictures emerge to fill out the vacant page.

Jonathan strains to make out what he is seeing. "It can't be! What the fuck is going on? What's happening to me? I am going crazy."

He looks closely at the images on the page.

"Is it Wolfman throwing his baby into the air"?

He focuses on the figure, which seems to come to life on the page and is moving off the page towards him.

"But Wolfman never had a gun," Jonathan shrieks as he hurls the files against the wall which make a thudding noise. The papers scatter in all directions.

He gets up to open the window. The cool breeze feels good on his face. He picks up the papers from the floor and sits down again to resume reading. He barely manages to get through one page when once again he stands up.

He is giddy and nauseous and feels a mild panic attack coming on. He stretches his arms in the air, drinks a glass of water and goes to the washroom. He fills up the washbasin with icy water and submerges his head in the water for a few seconds. He repeats this several times. He gulps down a valium and heads back to his office, tie loosened and hair disheveled. He shuts his office door, sets his alarm for fifteen minutes before the start of the meeting, puts his head on his desk and falls asleep almost immediately.

"It's clear," says Jonathan to the Wolfman team, "that our strategy here has to focus on diminished responsibility. The facts are clear and indisputable and beyond a reasonable doubt and even though Stevie says that he wants to be held fully accountable and deserves to be severely punished, our job as lawyers is to provide a defense for him which acknowledges that although he broke the law, he was not in a fit state of mind psychologically.

The amount of alcohol documented in his blood stream was way beyond the normal limits. It is clear that Stevie didn't plan to do what he did. Moe's death was not premeditated. Regrettably, in the court of public opinion he is guilty without any measure of doubt and people, amongst them some significant others, are calling for the death penalty to be reinstated in New York and shouting for Stevie to be put to death by lethal injection. We have to therefore keep our collective cool as lawyers and human beings and ensure that Stevie gets the best defense possible. I am not suggesting that we go with an insanity defense that could get Stevie acquitted. He is not after all suffering from any mental disorder – certainly not that I am aware of. Besides and here, I want to reference a Hebrew expression that is apropos: *maarit ayin* – literally translated as 'appearance of the eye', how things look, what is appropriate behavior. Trying to argue for an insanity defense will not only damage our credibility here as his defense team, but more important, the public at large will just not buy it. That's of course not the reason why we will not employ this strategy. Any good lawyer and legal team can build a strong case even with the flimsiest of material, but for me both personally and professionally, this would not be acceptable and I would not countenance it.

Justice has to be seen to be done. Any questions or comments? I value your input."

A World of Pains, Solly Kaplinski, 2015

Jonathan gets up to adjust the room temperature. He is feeling a sudden chill and begins to shiver.

"Jonathan", Mike, one of the interns began, "Let me shed another light on this insanity argument. Stevie's blood tests show that not only was he drinking heavily but also the amount consumed fell into the top percentile.

Could we not make a case that alcohol consumption not only substantially impaired his mental functioning but that when that terrible incident took place, I would like to respectfully suggest that Stevie was in fact insane - call it temporary insanity. Look, his record until this tragedy has been impeccable - not even a traffic violation!"

"Let's not go there, Mike. We have a compelling case here for involuntary manslaughter. Stevie did something terrible in the heat of the moment, his mind fueled by alcohol – not by insanity. He simply snapped under the circumstances. He was reckless and made an awful mistake. He needs to be punished but the law is about justice - not vengeance. He needs to serve time and then hopefully rehabilitate himself and find his place back in society although this tragedy will haunt him for the rest of his life. Wherever he goes, because of his fame - now infamy, he will be identified with this dastardly crime.

I can tell you that one of my former very high profile clients, who murdered his wife in a fit of passion, and was imprisoned for several years and then released after a belated confession, found no rest and was forced to live in the shadows. His punishment was a very public and unmerciful one. Whenever he went to a restaurant or to a movie, there would be a sudden hush and all eyes would be turned on him. I remember meeting him soon after his release for lunch at an elegant downtown hotel but out of view from the public eye - in a private room. He had to enter and leave the hotel through a side entrance.

Eventually he had to leave the country in order to build a new life for himself.

Think also of O. J. Simpson and yes, he is now in jail but prior to his acquittal in his criminal trial, he had no respite from people who jeered at and tormented him whenever he was in the public arena.

Similarly with Stevie: he will probably be forced to live furtively in the margins - and if identified, in the spotlight. It's a never – ending punishment."

Doctor Max Bromberg's office: September 18, 1996

"Jonathan, I want to come back to what we discussed last week. You feel that somehow your emotions regarding Wolfman are possibly clouding your objectivity and judgment as a legal practitioner. I want to focus on this today since I think we may be getting to the heart of your anxiety here.

And today, I want you to lie on the couch."

Jonathan gets up from the easy chair and stretches out on the couch.

"I want to zoom in especially on the images of the child that you have seen. I want you to concentrate and try to block everything else out except the child. I need you to take a deep breath and to be relaxed and at ease. Can you do that for me?

I also want you to close your eyes and try to switch off from everything else.

What I am going to do with your permission, Jonathan, is to hypnotize you. Hypnosis is, in professional hands, a harmless procedure. It is often used by specialists to help clients cope with anxiety. In your case, I want to use it in order to calm you. I can see that you are in a distressed space.

Hypnosis can also help recall past memories. I believe that what you are feeling may be connected in some way to a past experience.

Are you ok with this?"

"I trust you completely, Max. I feel safe with you. I feel comfortable going down this road."

"Jonathan, I also need to tell you that if I am correct and there is a link between what happened in your past and your current agitated state, what may emerge could be potentially painful and damaging.

Forgetting the past, which we often do, is sometimes a way to defend and protect ourselves from terrifying and horrific events that we experienced - and the emotions and memories associated with those events.

Take away this defense mechanism of forgetting or 'blocking out' and we would be utterly helpless and crack under the unbearable strain of this flood of past volatile emotional experiences overflowing into our consciousness.

I hope I'm not being too technical."

"I think I understand. Please continue Max."

"I must point out, however, that sometimes what may be remembered under hypnosis - even vividly, may not be fully

A World of Pains, Solly Kaplinski, 2015

accurate and worst case scenario, sometimes never happened. There have been for example, traumatic cases where women's repressed memories around sexual assault or child abuse - sometimes by their fathers, never took place - with disastrous consequences as you can well imagine. We are therefore operating in a zone that may be unreliable.

If by the way, at any stage, you feel that what you are undergoing, what's coming up to the surface is too threatening, to anxiety provoking, we can stop the process immediately."

Jonathan is stretched out on the couch and is already in a light trance but not asleep. He is aware of his surroundings as he listens to Max's soothing voice.

Pachelbel's Canon plays in the background in a continuous loop.

"Jonathan, let your body relax. Try to shut out the world around you. The only thing you should hear is the beautiful soft music."

Jonathan is quiet for several minutes. All that can be heard is his labored breathing.

The silence punctuated by the lilting melody continues...

Max looks at the relaxed body of Jonathan and with some trepidation, proceeds.

"Try if you can to recall the infant that you have seen. Can you perhaps describe him? Maybe there are some distinguishing features? Jonathan, when you are ready, tell me what you see."

There is another prolonged silence. Pachelbel seems to fill the space.

"I think... it looks like... a young boy, no, an infant, possibly with dark hair. The baby is crying - perhaps even screaming. A piercing, painful cry, almost like the sound of a wounded animal." Jonathan presses his hands tightly around his ears.

And then he lets go gently.

"For some reason", he continues, "the baby seems, it's not exactly clear, is it possible, to be hurtling through the air?

I also hear another loud cry, screeching, beseeching, and pleading. It's a woman's voice. She seems to be lying on the damp, rain-soaked ground, practically naked. Her contorted face also looks somewhat familiar but... her endless tears mar her features. There is also a panicked expression on her face. Oh my God! She knows she's about to die."

"This may be hard to do Jonathan but can you see anything else?"

"I am not certain but I think there seems to be, can there be another figure in this picture – possibly a man but he is almost a complete blur, very hazy, not recognizable? He also has something in his hand ....which could possibly be, I am not sure, a weapon."

"How do you know it's a male?"

Jonathan sits up with a jolt. "I think we need to stop now."

Doctor Max Bromberg in session with Doctor Frances Clore: September 25, 1996

"Frances, how many years have I been in therapy with you coming to seek your guidance on my cases – is it twenty? I am dealing with a case now that I think is unique. My patient is to all intents and purposes a highly successful lawyer and human rights campaigner, happily married to a person who is also very successful in her career with two super intelligent sons. I find it strange that he has not let on to his wife that he is seeing me but I will let that go for the meantime. It's his choice.

I have had several sessions with him revolving around images of baby children being thrown into the air. These images it seems have been set off by his involvement in the horrific Wolfman case.

If my intuition is correct, I believe there may be a link between these images he has seen or dreamt of and the Wolfman incident. And I believe that as this unfolds, and it may do so very quickly, it's possible that my client himself is either directly or indirectly involved in a similar situation."

"Is there anything in his history which reinforces your possible suspicions?"

"Not at this stage. He was born in Kaunas before the war, came from a working class family, and somehow got very involved during the worst excesses of the Holocaust in helping a Jewish family – a mother and daughter, hide from the Nazis.

He subsequently made his way to America with them, converted to Judaism, married the daughter and has made an outstanding success of his life especially given his very humble and modest beginnings here in America as an impoverished immigrant: clueless, penniless and barely literate in the English language."

"So what makes this case unique, Max?"

Max pours himself some iced lemonade freshly prepared by Frances and drinks almost the full glass before he continues.

"Frances, we have often spoken about repressed memories,

A World of Pains, Solly Kaplinski, 2015

especially the sensational case which made the headlines not so long ago involving the teacher who supposedly raped one of his students."

"You are referring to the Lestere case where the student, B, accused her teacher Mitchell Lestere of raping her some ten years after the fact?"

"Yes - on the strength of supposed long repressed memories which suddenly emerged while the troubled girl was undergoing psychotherapy."

"Well, we know that this was thrown out of court and Lestere was found not guilty although his good name and reputation will forever be tarnished. However, Max, I am still not sure where you are going with this? We know that there are repressed memory cases which have proven to be legitimate but what makes your case unique?"

"Frances, repressed memories always seem to emerge from the victims of so called abuse. It is a rare occurrence for the perpetrator to suddenly remember something traumatic from the past. I have the strong feeling that this is where my case is going to end up."

"Max, you are treading on difficult terrain here. On the one hand, the literature does indicate that the experience of traumatic events may be so overwhelming that in order to cope in the here and now, somehow, the traumas are compartmentalized, or to use a computer analogy, a firewall is created which protects the person. It's as if the person's identity is divided or somehow carved off and the traumatic events are frozen or embedded in the unconscious - sometimes permanently, or until for whatever reason, these painful memories may emerge over time into the present.

Perhaps it's repression or denial or avoidance – or even malingering that's kept them long buried. Who after all wants to be faced with the unpleasant, the frightening, the humiliating, and the embarrassing truth? We all have a strong need to protect ourselves.

On the other hand, as you know, it may be difficult to tease out the differences between the actual events and the memories we hold of those events especially if this took place so many years ago. This does not mean that the event did not take place or that it was not horrific or traumatic but the field of understanding of memory – especially going back over a long time, is fraught with obstacles and is complex.

It also bears repeating that old memories may also be influenced by subsequent experiences that we have which can filter or shape those memories of the past. It may therefore

A World of Pains, Solly Kaplinski, 2015

become difficult to separate fact from fiction. And what may emerge from these past experiences could - worst case scenario, be false memories."

Frances pauses for a few minutes to look out of her office window that has an unobstructed view of Central Park. The spectacular fall foliage always inspires her. Max is familiar with this ritual. He knows that Frances is deep in thought, weighing up all the options. And because he values her professional expertise and guidance, he indulges her by remaining silent.

"On reflection however, from what you have told me about your client, I think that you should step up the frequency of seeing him. I would advise two to three sessions per week. He is going to need you desperately. He probably does already – especially since he's not unburdening with his wife."

Doctor Bromberg's office: September 30 to October 30, 1996

Jonathan is now seeing Max twice a week. He is dizzy and nauseous and has shooting pains in his face especially as he painstakingly tries to unfold the scene of the infant being thrown into the air.

"I know this is difficult Jonathan, but try to tell me what you are seeing."

"It's so hard to make this out but it seems that someone is laughing hysterically... and it looks like there is a young woman lying at his feet ...somehow she is familiar.... she... she is sobbing and clinging onto him so tightly that he cannot move... he almost feels suffocated. He is rooted to the ground. Max ...I...I can't go on...I can't breathe...I need to stop for a few minutes."

"Jonathan, I know you are in pain but I think we are making progress. When you feel you can, please try to continue. There is no pressure of time. I have no appointments following our session."

Jonathan's head is throbbing and he feels an immense pressure on his chest.

"Max, there seems to be a sort of fog, a haze, but I think I can make out what appears to be a deep pit and it looks like ....I can't believe this ... no I can't ...there are bodies piled up on top of each other, many bodies. Christ, this is Picasso's Guernica. People are naked holding hands standing around the edge of a pit. They have the look of death on their faces. Dogs are barking, shots are fired. The noise is unbearable. And many young men are deliriously happy.

A World of Pains, Solly Kaplinski, 2015

Am I dreaming this Dante's Inferno or is it real?"

Jonathan lapses into silence. His chest is heaving as he struggles to control his breathing.

Ten minutes pass by.

Jonathan's body visibly shakes as if he were experiencing mild convulsions.

"Max, this is just too much for me ... a baby's body is somehow flying through the air and lands into the pit. How can it be? What is going on Max? Please help me. I can't take this anymore." He is sobbing.

Max gets up from his chair and takes Jonathan's hand. He grips it tightly. With his other hand, he uses a Kleenex to dab away the sweat on Jonathan's forehead.

"Max, I see someone else whose face is also familiar, who is laughing uncontrollably. He...he has a rifle in his hand and is firing shots at a rapid pace. Oh my God - he is using the butt of the rifle to savagely beat the woman who is at his feet."

"Jonathan, can you identify this person?"

Jonathan is pale and unable to speak. He feels numb, almost in shock. Without warning, he slumps in his chair seemingly passing out. Max jumps up and pours some cold water on his face which revives him.

Max orders a cab for Jonathan. When he returns home, he is weary to the world. He has virtually no energy to walk up the stairs to the bedroom. His breathing is rapid and shallow and he is highly agitated.

Unable to undress, he collapses on the bed. "Sandra", he can barely whisper, "my mouth is parched. I need iced water - desperately. I have sharp pains in my chest. I think I'm having a heart attack." She immediately phones the emergency services who dispatch an ambulance. Sandra also calls her close friend, Justin Saxe, a cardiac specialist who rushes to the Varnas home almost immediately. He does a thorough examination of Jonathan, who is fully conscious. He sits him in an easy chair, loosens his clothing and wraps a blanket around him. He checks his rate of breathing and then again every five minutes. He feels the pulse - the blood pressure seems to be normal. Jonathan is breathing with difficulty and he is wheezing. He again asks for water but Saxe tells him to wait. He doesn't want to give him any liquids in order to prevent inhalation of vomit.

To Sandra's relief, Saxe tells her that Jonathan has suffered a shock but not a major one and that he prescribes a week's rest at home but under close supervision. He tells her that it is probably a combination of stress and hard work coupled with the anxiety of the Wolfman trial that has brought this on.

Sandra dispenses with the ambulance when it arrives soon thereafter.

Jonathan falls into a deep sleep and appears almost dead to the world. Approximately 18 hours later, he awakes. Sandra and the boys are at his bedside. He smiles faintly at them. "We thought we had lost you, Jonathan," she cries as she hugs and kisses him.

"Jonathan, I have given this a lot of thought especially over the last day and a half. I know this is going to be hard for you to hear knowing how utterly dedicated and committed you are to your work and to your clients. Please hear me out. I honestly think you need to give some thought to retiring. You have worked unbelievably hard all your life. You have given of yourself relentlessly. I am concerned that you are running on empty. I need you now more than ever. We still have some good years ahead of us and we have so much to look forward to together. I don't ask much of you but do this for me Jonathan, for our boys. Please, I am begging you..."

The Varnas home: October 30, 1996

An early morning call wakes up the Varnas household. The Norwegian Ambassador to the US tells Jonathan that he will shortly be receiving a call from Oslo and that he should keep the line open.

Several hours later, the Chair of the Norwegian Nobel Committee informs him that he is the winner of the 1996 Nobel Peace Prize for his contribution to human rights, democracy and peace.

The excitement in the Varnas home is overwhelming. Visitors come streaming in; all the phones are ringing with congratulatory messages. The President also calls Jonathan and tells him how proud he is not only that an American has won the Nobel Peace Prize but also a man of Jonathan's stature and gravitas brings honor to the prize itself.

Sandra hopes that this wonderful news will lift Jonathan since his mood following the shock has been somewhat dulled. He now seems to be more animated and lively and returns almost to his former self. But Sandra can see that the glint in his eye has gone, that Jonathan is a shadow of his former self and she can't put a finger on why. She has a strong feeling though that things will never be the same again.

A World of Pains, Solly Kaplinski, 2015

Jonathan is still unable to reveal to Sandra that he has been in therapy now almost three times a week.

Doctor Max Bromberg in session with Doctor Frances Clore: November 10, 1996

"Frances, just to recap: Jonathan is in therapy because he has recurring visions of the scene in which it appears that a woman and her child are murdered. It seems that the Wolfman case has been the trigger for these revelations.

These frightening visions, blurry at first, have with hypnotherapy over the last few weeks, started to fill out to the point where I believe that at any time now, as unbelievable and as shocking as it may seem, he will recognize that he committed brutal and savage murders.

These gruesome and dastardly deeds, which have been repressed for a few decades, will obviously come as a major shock to him.

I am anxious about how best to proceed here. I am especially concerned that in his clearly fragile state, these revelations will push him over the edge.

You have been my clinical supervisor all these years and your guidance and supervision have always been invaluable and given me the confidence to deal with the most difficult of cases - both long and short term. The Varnas case however is in a class of its own and I am not sure if I can cope. What do you think?"

"Max, you have already increased the frequency of the sessions during the week. Varnas trusts you and is clearly leaning on you to see him through what is probably the most difficult emotional crisis he has ever had to confront.

His ghastly and traumatic past that he is unaware of is going to be revealed to him. Through you, the lock to his seemingly impermeable memory door is likely going to be pried open and a nightmare of unbelievable proportions could follow."

Frances stands up, takes a deep breath, opens the window, and pours coffee for both of them.

"There are several scenarios here Max. Firstly, acute depression may set in. Here is a person who has reached the pinnacle of his career - the Nobel Peace Prize and all the status, awe and respect it confers on him - only to have his past exposed and explode. This will reveal him to possibly be a murderer – and in the process, bring the secure world that

A World of Pains, Solly Kaplinski, 2015

he currently inhabits and masters, crashing down on him and his family.

Realizing the sheer horror of what he did and the implications for him with his family, friends and peers and legally, he could also experience a psychotic episode where he literally loses his mind and suffers a breakdown as a way of coping with his situation."

Frances is deep in thought for a few moments. Max is restless and fidgeting awkwardly in his chair.

"Jonathan could," Francis continues, "vacillate between utter shame, self - loathing, confusion, terror and may be unable to function normally. He could break down irretrievably and disintegrate in your very presence. The psychoses could, therefore, be of longer duration where he is lost forever in mental illness.

The challenge here is how to give him a safe space to confront his past.

And given the magnitude of the despicable horrors that have been buried, locked and hidden that will presently, it seems, come rushing to the surface, is it possible for him through you to safely confront his past and more importantly, himself?
Can it be done?
How he will cope is impossible to predict. I also believe that your client is at profound risk for suicidal behavior."

"In that case, if he is a danger to himself, should I commit him to hospitalization? Do I let his wife know? She is completely in the dark. He may need to be protected."

"Max, I don't know what to tell you. Jonathan trusts you completely. You are his anchor, his hope, and at this stage his only source of comfort and sustenance. This is a judgment call here and I am afraid your options are limited. Timing is also an issue."

"Frances, I also need to tell you that I am deeply conflicted. If I am in fact in the presence of someone who has committed murders, I am ethically bound to report this to the authorities. Yes, I know there is psychiatrist - patient privilege and that I need to honor and to respect confidentiality between doctor and client. This is a sacred principle in our practice but how do I deal with this? What am I supposed to do here Frances?"

"This is a painful dilemma Max. If you proceed, who do you report this to? More than fifty years have passed since these crimes were committed. Does this fall into the category of war crimes? Does the statute of limitations apply here? I am afraid I am of no help to you on this. But bear in mind that you still don't know for sure that he is a murderer. It all seems to point in that direction but who knows what else may emerge in your on-going sessions with him.

A World of Pains, Solly Kaplinski, 2015

What I am more confident in telling you is that as the truth emerges for Jonathan – whatever it may be, I know that you will be non - judgmental and allow him to experience and feel the painful truth about himself in the belief that with your unconditional support, he is able to survive these gruesome revelations."

Without warning, Max suddenly stands up and slams his fist against the wall. One of the family photographs is dislodged. There are shards of glass on the floor. A few books fall from the bookcase.

"Frances, I...I don't need all this shit in my life. I am at the stage now where I am beginning to resent Jonathan.

I am pissed off with this son of a bitch. I am dealing with a fucking murderer. I am sure of this. I don't think I can or even want to continue seeing him. I almost want to strangle this bastard."

"Max, whatever feelings you may have about Jonathan, you have to be able to hold it together for him. You can't reject him now. He has no one else.

It is understandable that you are angry, resentful and disgusted and that you want to hurt him. How can you not be touched by what is about to happen and what may have happened so many years ago?

You may want to scream violently as the curtain is slowly pulled back and the Pandora's Box of evil is pried open - and Satan emerges. But you can't scream.

Only silently."

Frances passes Max a tray of cookies. He stuffs a handful into his mouth. He knows he needs a sugar rush at times like this. He gulps them down too quickly, starts coughing, almost choking. Frances pours him a glass of water.

"Max, as much as your moral center is pushed off balance and as much as you want to let your emotions go, you need to be there for Jonathan, to be his anchor, his support, his pathway to possible recovery and saving himself - as difficult as it may be.

I guess the bottom line is that while you will obviously be concerned that the emergence of the truth could seriously endanger Jonathan's life, you will somehow need to find a way to hold out a lifeline to him no matter how flimsy, a ray of hope that there is a bridge to deliverance, however narrow it may be.

It will be his commitment to this road of redemption, whatever that may emerge to be, that keeps him alive, sane and functional and begins gently to move him away from the overwhelming pain, horror and shame that no sane person can continue to endure.

My dear friend and esteemed colleague who I admire and respect, I know that it's a long, lonely road out there but you are not on your own. I am here for you."

Doctor Bromberg's office: December 1, 1996

"Max, I need to tell you that I am calling a halt to our sessions. I have the Nobel Peace Prize ceremony in ten days and I am going to the airport straight from this session. I need to make arrangements and more important, to prepare my acceptance speech to which I have already given a lot of thought.

To continue with the therapy now would add almost unbearably to my stress levels. I know you are deeply concerned but believe me, I am on top of things. I am highly motivated and when I get back from Oslo, we will resume our sessions."

Max tries to prevail upon Jonathan to continue the sessions for the remaining week before the Nobel ceremony, stressing that the situation is too delicate to abandon at this stage, that they have reached almost a climax in their therapeutic relationship, that he is worried that left incomplete and without support, Jonathan's situation could deteriorate ....and rapidly.

"Max, I appreciate your genuine concern for me and I thank you profusely but I can't continue at this stage. I know what I have to do."

"Jonathan, does your wife know what's going on?"

"I forbid you under any circumstances to say a word to her about our sessions."

Max fears for the worst.

On his way to the airport, Jonathan calls Stevie Wolfman at Rikers.

"Stevie, I know you will be surprised by this unscheduled call but I want to let you know that firstly, I owe you an enormous debt of gratitude. Your honesty and expressions of remorse and your wanting so desperately to be accountable for what happened, have helped me more than you will ever know.

Secondly, while this will come as a shock to you and I apologize profusely to you, I will no longer be representing you. I can't explain why - you will soon find out. But rest assured, my firm will continue to represent you and prepare the best possible defense for you."

Before a shocked Stevie can reply, Jonathan hangs up.

A World of Pains, Solly Kaplinski, 2015

Oslo: December 10, 1996

The ceremony for the Nobel Prize for Peace takes place in Norway unlike ceremonies for the other Nobel Prizes that are awarded in Stockholm. Alfred Nobel apparently believed that since Norway was rarely involved in modern times in war, it would be more fitting and especially symbolic for the Peace Prize to be presented in the city of peace.

Oslo in the winter despite the freezing temperatures is magical. Surrounded by forests it is a paradise with frozen fjords, crisp, cold air and snow laden streets. Travel brochures describe the city as wonderful and romantic, "a break from the norm" and ideal to get away from it all.

The Oslo City Hall (rådhus) is one of Oslo's most famous buildings. It was decorated by great Norwegian artists from the 1900-1950 period with motifs from Norwegian history, culture and working life.

On this day, it is filled to capacity with almost a thousand VIPs and guests in addition to press and television teams.

Jonathan Varnas is seated near the podium together with the Nobel Committee and its permanent secretary. Members of the Royal Family are also present as they are every year maintaining a tradition that goes back to 1905.

In the rows of seats behind the Royal Family are seated representatives of the Government, the Diplomatic Corps and other specially invited guests.

The chairperson of the Norwegian Nobel Committee opens up the proceedings:

"It is my privilege and honor to introduce to you this year's Nobel Peace Prize winner – Jonathan Varnas. Mr. Varnas is awarded the prize for his fearless and courageous dedication to children's rights, for standing up to injustice on their behalf, for fighting with every ounce of his body and every breath to protect them – nationally and internationally.

Whether it's children abused in their homes, or schools, or being exploited in the work place, or children who are forced into prostitution or who are malnourished and left to die, whether it's children who have curable diseases who require elementary health care or children who have become refugees, Mr. Varnas has led the charge - on public platforms, at the United Nations and in the many articles he has published both in the journals or via the media; he has been at the forefront. He has been a trailblazer.

I need not remind you how he almost singlehandedly took on the challenge of ensuring that children who are orphans, victims of aids and war victims, are provided with all the

A World of Pains, Solly Kaplinski, 2015

comforts possible in the more than fifty Varnas Compassion Centers for Children he has established around the world.

He has also ensured that these Centers are staffed by dedicated professionals of the highest caliber who tend to all their needs.

Mr. Varnas especially drew attention to the perpetrators of crimes against children by insisting that even many years after the Holocaust, the blood of children still cried out for justice. Mr. Varnas became their voice – loud, strident and forceful - but dignified.

Mr. Varnas, I ask you to come forward to be presented with the Nobel Diploma and the Nobel Medal."

Jonathan comes up to the podium, looks at the audience all around him, feels the glare of the lights, adjusts the microphone and takes out his prepared speech. He drinks a glass of water, clears his throat, looks at Sandra seated just a few rows away who gives him an encouraging smile and whispers to him:

"I love you forever."

Ruben and David are bursting with pride.

"Members of the academy," he begins, "let me first say how grateful I am to all of you for giving me this award, the Nobel Peace Prize. This is perhaps the greatest recognition and ultimate reward one can attain for one's professional endeavors and I would like so much to accept this unparalleled honor.

The most generous monetary gift that accompanies this award will hopefully all be given to the Varnas Compassion Centers for Children."

Jonathan's mouth is dry. He pours himself another glass of water from the porcelain jug on the podium and drinks it slowly.

He is conscious of all eyes fixed on him and the unbearably loud silence. He feels faint and fatigued but pushes himself to continue.

"I need though to share something with you that as you will see, will make it impossible for me to accept this award. I know this will come as a shock to all of you sitting in this hall and to my family and friends, and to the tens of thousands who are watching this live on television or via the internet.

What I am about to say will jolt you but I beg you, I implore you, please allow me to say what I want to say, to say what I need to say before you respond – in any form or fashion."

There is an audible gasp from the audience but no one moves. It is as if they are frozen in their seats. Almost catatonic.

A World of Pains, Solly Kaplinski, 2015

"The story begins more than fifty years ago on October 25th 1942 in a wooded countryside area less than ten miles from the center of Vilnius in Lithuania, the Ponar forest. It used to be a popular holiday and picnic resort, a place of tranquility and peace in the lush woods.

A paved road and railroad connect Ponar to the city today as it did then.

At Ponar, a fuel storage facility had been under construction to serve the nearby airbase. Massive pits had been excavated for fuel tanks. The pits were connected by ditches but were never completed for their original purpose.

Instead, unbelievably, they were used for the extermination of tens of thousands of people. 70 000 Jews from Vilnius and surrounding townships as well as thousands of Poles and Russians were murdered there by the Nazis and their Lithuanian collaborators. Men, women and children were shot at the edge of the pits and then buried in them after being covered with slaked lime.

Executions by shootings continued there for three years from June 1941 until July 1944.

Ponar became one of several sites of mass murder and large-scale massacres in Eastern Europe, and the final resting place of the Jews of Vilnius.

I remember the day as if it were yesterday. The weather was chilly although the sun was shining sporadically. There were clouds overhead and at times, an occasional drizzle.

I arrived at Ponar early morning on October 25, 1942. There were all sorts of rumors about what was happening at Ponar and I was curious to know what was going on. Chozanda my friend greeted me warmly. He had already been at Ponar for more than a week and asked me to join him. Chozanda and I had studied in the same elementary school.

It was clear when I saw him that he was unsteady on his feet, swaying from side to side – obviously in a state of intoxication. He beckoned me to one of the kitchens where there were dozens of huge pots of vodka. Between the two of us, we must have consumed several liters and gulped mouthfuls of special tablets (they called them wonder drugs) before we proceeded outside. I knew I was inebriated but looking back on these many, many years that have passed, I also felt like I was still fully in control.

Chozanda in his drunken stupor told me that what I was about to experience would be like nothing else in my life – sheer ecstasy and joy since the main sport at Ponar was killing Jews.

Chozanda in fact belonged to a group called the Shaulists, young Lithuanians aged seventeen to twenty five whose primary task was to operate the firing squads at Ponar. They had all enthusiastically volunteered to help the Nazis.

Passing me a rifle, we went out into the cold sunlight and made our way to one of the pits. I immediately saw a group of about ten to fifteen men in blindfolds, all naked, holding one another's hands and marching in single file, led by someone whom I immediately recognized – Jurgis, who was a few years older than me and who lived in my neighborhood.

Jurgis led the group to the edge of the pit. Chozanda joined the firing squad. He asked me to join him but I didn't feel comfortable. I observed the armed men joking amongst themselves and then without warning opened fire. The blindfolded men fell into the pit. Any of them who showed any signs of life, were shot again.

I could see in the distance another group, this time women, being marched naked to the pit. This carried on for a few hours with bodies being piled on top of each other in the pit. Any signs of life, any whimpering, moans or cries for help alerted conscientious Shaulists who took careful aim and fired off rounds of bullets to ensure that there were no survivors. Still I did not participate.

Even when Chozanda and his partners receive money, valuables and clothes of the victims, and after a celebration "victory" meal with unlimited liquor - and participation at a special mass to honor the occasion, I could not bring myself to join in."

There is not a sound from the audience who are spell bound, hanging on to every word from Jonathan.

Sandra is fighting to hold back tears. Anger and dismay are etched on the boys' faces.

"Later as I joined Chozanda's group to drink more vodka and consume more drugs, I felt more relaxed and at ease.

I became less inhibited, especially when we spoke about the Jews and how evil they were, how they were robbing our beloved country and were accumulating wealth at our expense.

I also recalled all those lessons in Sunday school when our teachers told us how the Jews had crucified Christ. And I recalled my own father's words,

'The Jews are our misfortune - *Die Juden sind unser Unglück!* The only good Jew is a dead Jew!'

Anger in me welled up and truth be told, I could not wait for the next round of killing Jews. And I, like the rest of my newfound friends, opened up fire with relish.

Another group arrives at our pit – they have come straight off the train that brought them from Vilnius to Ponar - men, women and children. They are ordered to undress. They know what is about to happen. They plead, they beg, they cry. We are unmoved. We beat them and they undress. We force them to the edge of the pit and shoot them from the back of their heads and they fall into the pit. I am without emotion, a cold, heartless killer – even when the man I shoot... when his skull opens up and his brains and blood are splattered on my face and on my clothes."

People begin to stand up in the hall and attempt to walk towards the exits. Jonathan raises his voice,

"Please sit down - immediately, and I must insist: no talking. Not a word." As if in a mass hypnosis, they shuffle back to their seats - in silence.

"If you don't mind, I will continue. I know this is not easy for you to hear all this but I won't keep you for long. I promise. Thank you for your patience."

Jonathan is amazed at how malleable they are, almost like putty in his hands.

"And", Jonathan continues softly, "I remember this particular incident clearly: One of the Shaulists pulls a child out from under the piled clothing and then another...and another. The mothers in their desperation had tried to conceal their babies - to no avail. The children are thrown into the pit and shot.

All the clothing from the undressed victims in the pile will later be sold at the market.

As we start leaving the pit, I see by chance a familiar face, a young woman my age with a child suckling at her breast. Rachel Braude was in my class at school. We were next-door neighbors. Her father, a doctor, treated my family when we were ill and her mother looked after me, even baby-sat on occasion.

I don't know what got into me but I was in an uncontrollable rage, even as she pleads with me to spare her and her child. It was if all the normal superego controls were entirely absent from my being. To me she was just another filthy Jew, a sub-human who was sucking up the air. I honestly don't know what drove me but I simply had to get rid of her and her child.

I threw the child into the air towards the pit and both Chozanda and I shot simultaneously as if we were shooting at clay pigeons. The baby fell lifeless to the ground. But I didn't, I couldn't stop there. Rachel was still at my feet, whimpering, even though I had hit her several times with my rifle butt.

A World of Pains, Solly Kaplinski, 2015

One more time I said to myself and that will be the end of her forever. With all the strength I can muster, I smash her head so hard, it is literally torn off from the shoulders and it lolls around like a bloodied football. Chozanda is laughing hysterically and attempts to kick the head as if he were playing in a soccer game.

And I," whispers Jonathan, barely audible, "I...I join him."

People in the audience make another attempt to walk towards the exits. Some are crying; others are screaming.

"I know this is very upsetting," says Jonathan raising his voice, "but please, I need to finish. Stay with me. I am almost done."

The King of Norway, the much loved and deeply revered monarch, who together with his wife is always present at the Nobel Peace Prize ceremony slowly stands up. All eyes turn to him. There is a deathly silence.

"Let the man finish," he says in a deep, booming voice. He gestures to the professionals of the national security services who are standing around the perimeter of the hall not to take any action. The King resumes his seat.

Jonathan feels the anger of the audience welling up, and the shame, but nobody moves. They are rooted to the spot. The silence is deafening. "And then", he continues quietly, "I consume as many liters of vodka as I can possibly imbibe until my body and my brain can't take it anymore. And I pass out - and the memories of that day become obliterated, wiped out, buried deep in the furthest recesses of my mind, repressed and denied. Blocked out maybe because of the alcohol and the drugs or the horror of the evil deeds or a combination of the two... but all this revealed to me just few days ago via my psychotherapist." Jonathan removes a handkerchief from his pocket to dry the tears, which are streaming down his cheek.

"And so I stand before you today as a despicable specimen, clearly an unworthy candidate for surely the greatest honor of all that that can be bestowed - the Nobel Peace Prize.

I deliberated long and hard about whether I should have declined it before this prestigious ceremony. I felt though that if my life has to have any meaning at all, it should be through a confession of my sins on a global platform with an audience of thousands of viewers via TV and the internet and of course you, the audience with me.

Had I discussed this with my wife, a Justice of the New York Supreme Court, who it pains me to say is hearing this for the first time with you and the rest of my family – such is my shame, embarrassment and guilt, she would have said to me, I

A World of Pains, Solly Kaplinski, 2015

am sure, 'Jonathan, you are not the same person today that you were more than fifty years ago. There is a case here for mitigating circumstances, you were under the influence of alcohol; you couldn't have been responsible for your wicked deeds. Then you were Yonas, a callow, inebriated youth; today you are Jonathan, an upright person of character, deeply respected, loved and admired for your holy work, a Nobel Laureate.'

Yonas and Jonathan, Jonathan and Yonas, two sides of the same coin – a truly bad penny. How I wish I could excise him, amputate this phantom limb from my being. If only he never existed – my evil twin joined to me at the hip. But alas, I am Yonas and he is me."

His gaze turns towards Sandra who is slumped like a rag doll on her chair, as if to remonstrate with her.

"For far too long, we in the legal profession have used the argument of mitigating circumstances to allow criminals not to be held accountable for their criminal behaviors. This path is not for me. I believe that I need to be punished for what I did – no matter the good I may have done in later years.

Yes, I fought to protect vulnerable and helpless children for most of my adult life. Yes, I was their champion and advocate – and their voice. All my sacred deeds, however, cannot undo for a moment the fact that I murdered innocent people, a mother and her child amongst them, and what's worse, people whom I…I knew. I wasn't just a bystander but a perpetrator, a vicious murderer.

Unlike those who maimed, tortured and killed and who gave testimony to the Truth and Reconciliation Commission in South Africa about their crimes committed during the horrific apartheid era in South Africa in order to gain amnesty, honored guests, ladies and gentlemen, let me be absolutely and unambiguously clear:

I am not asking for amnesty, absolution, nor for forgiveness.

Nothing can excuse the savage crimes that I committed and no one can forgive me - not the dead whose blood I have drenched on my hands and now so heavily on my conscience, or their descendants who cry out to the heavens for justice.

To apologize to them would be obscene - and an insult. For my ultimate disregard for the most basic of all human values: the preservation of human life, I must be punished - and severely. I cannot be forgiven at all - under any circumstances. This confessional to a worldwide audience and jury is so woefully inadequate to excuse me in any way.

Words of contrition, of remorse and regret cannot eliminate the evil of my deeds. They can however be a salutary lesson

A World of Pains, Solly Kaplinski, 2015

for the ages in bringing attention to how low man can stoop, how easy it is for him – for me, to become an animal in the wilds. A killer without a conscience. Oh how the mighty have fallen!"

Jonathan is parched. He feels his sweat drenched shirt clinging to his body. He fills up a glass of water and downs it in one gulp. He knows looking at the audience many of whom are weeping in their chairs, while others are standing ready to run for the exits, that he needs to conclude quickly.

"I am hopeful that if there is to be any redemption for me, it's that my confession will draw attention to a period in history where the laws of the jungle prevailed, where there were no laws in fact, where the beast ruled, where morality was a joke, where sadism was admired, where so called civilized people were seduced by and in love with death, and where murderers became role models to be respected, rewarded and emulated.

If the lessons of this tragedy can be learnt and applied, if people reflect authentically on the frailty and fragility of human life and how much it should be valued and dignified, I know that at the very least, my life will have had some value. But, I ask myself, what future is there for me in this world?

I have the mark of Cain on my head. I can no longer be part of a civilized community. The assassinated Prime Minister of Israel, Yitzhak Rabin a man who I admired so much condemned the murderer, Baruch Goldstein, who murdered twenty nine Palestinian worshippers referring to him as '... an errant weed ... a foreign implant...Sensible Judaism spits you out.' That's me. I am Goldstein. There is in reality only one way out for me – I have to be spat out."

Jonathan looks at Sandra one last time. She sits keeled over in her chair, motionless, eyes closed, the color drained from her face. Ruben and David sit expressionless not facing him, staring into the distance.

Out of the corner of his eyes, Jonathan sees security guards approaching him. He reaches into his suit pocket under his Nobel robes and whips out a gun. In a very measured and methodical way, Jonathan aims the gun in their direction. They freeze in their tracks. There are hysterical cries and shouts from the audience. People stand and rush for the exits.

Jonathan nervously fires a shot into the air, which hits one of the magnificent chandeliers overhead. The sound of the bullet and the shattered crystal glass crashing to the floor create a panic in the hall which is now almost in darkness.

In the ensuing pandemonium and chaos that breaks out, Jonathan storms out of the room, closes the doors tightly behind him, catches his breath and slowly but deliberately, he places the gun at his temple, and ever so gently, he squeezes the trigger.

Doctor Max Bromberg in session with Doctor Frances Clore: December 13, 1996

"Frances, I feel devastated for Jonathan's family and their pain and suffering. I am so stressed by his suicide. I think about it constantly and can't let it go.

I know that a number of psychiatrists have lost patients through suicide but I never imagined what angst they experienced. Perhaps I could have stopped him? I feel that I failed Jonathan. How am I going to face my colleagues? This is going to be with me for the rest of my life."

"Max, of course this is painful and stressful. You have been through an emotional upheaval. But I know that you cared so much for Jonathan and you 'held his hand' on a torturous journey. You were his pillar of strength and had a 'therapist love' for him. I am not sure what else you could have done."

"I… I feel so wasted, so depleted… everything is an effort. And as exhausted as I feel, I can't sleep. I don't want to leave my apartment and have not taken any calls. I feel so isolated, so alone."

"You are also grieving, you are in mourning for him … it's going to take time to heal."

"Should I take a break for a while Frances? Do I need this in my life? I've got a dead person on my hands."

"Max, you have been treating patients for more than thirty years and you have a stellar reputation. Yes, this is difficult period and you will continue to be in emotional pain. You've been through a nightmare and your self- confidence has taken a huge hit. But rest assured I will continue to work with you on the road to recovery and you will get there. You are not mourning alone.

In the meantime, as hard as this is, and please hear me out, you may want to consider making a *shiva* call to the family during their week of mourning, to pay your condolences, to offer your support."

"That's absurd Frances! That's absolute crap. Have you lost your mind? They don't even know that I exist. And when I divulge to them who I am, that I tried to help him, they will blame me for what happened. I can't do this! I can't face them. You are expecting too much of me."

"Max, you need to get a hold of yourself. This is not about you and believe me, I am not minimizing your pain and grief and how you feel. This is about his wife and sons. They have been shattered and are in deep mourning. They have just lost a husband and father in the most shocking circumstances. They probably need you more than you - and they will ever know... and you, you need them!"

The Varnas home: December 15, 1996

During the *shiva* week, Sandra is inconsolable. Ruben and David barely emerge from their rooms. The Varnas home is inundated with family, friends and colleagues who have come to commiserate, to share in their grief.

Sandra has not changed her torn blouse since the funeral.

The ritual of the *keriah*, the deliberate tearing of the garment, is not only an expression of deep pain and intense mourning; it is also a metaphor for a torn heart. Sandra is unable to engage with anyone. She is sprawled on a low chair in the crowded living room surrounded by people who are silent, waiting to take their cues from her.

Letters of condolence arrive from all over the world including one stamped from The Grand Hotel, Oslo, dated before the Nobel ceremony. Sandra recognizes the handwriting and with trembling hands, tears open the envelope.

"Sandrina my love, I can't imagine how difficult this must be for you, the pain and humiliation, the anger and embarrassment. My words will not comfort you nor be able to provide you with any measure of consolation and healing. But know this: I have always loved you. From the moment I first saw you in Kanas's office, wide-eyed, petrified and so afraid, I knew then that I wanted to protect you forever.

You were my first love, my only love.

I don't know why but as I sit in this lonely hotel room thinking of you and struggling with what to say in my confused emotional state, of the many joyful memories that come back of our lives together, what stands out is a song I composed as I slowly became proficient in the English language, clumsily expressing my passionate love for you.

'The thing that I fear most is losing you
Like a baby bird in its nest stranded all alone
I'd no longer see light I'd just wither and die
Like a flower whose petals close up in the night.

161

My whole life revolves around you babe

All the steps that I take embrace thoughts of you

You paint up my life you color my world

I am your canvas and you are my artist

Complete me

You inspire me fire me make my life whole

The sea is so great and my boat is so small

Sail me'

Sandra, my feelings for you today are as intense as they were so many years ago. This is so deeply painful.

My precious, my one and only - you were my rock and my anchor. But I have let you and our sons down so badly. I have caused you all irreparable harm and damage.

What I did as a young man was despicable, disgraceful and unforgivable and self-inflicted justice, death, was the only way out for me.

I can't expect you to understand this. But I need to explain to you why it has come to this tragic ending.

I was never able to comprehend why after so many years had passed since the Holocaust, I had not come across one incident of a killer, a murderer, a perpetrator spontaneously acknowledging his atrocious crimes and being prepared to be punished to the fullest extent possible. If anything, such animals continued to vehemently deny culpability and to disown the blood on their hands.

What's in their hearts we can never tell but supposing we give them the benefit of the doubt for a moment? Suppose that their deeds are so horrific that the mind blanks out, shuts down. What happens when they, like me, remember their ghastly crimes? Do they wake up in a cold sweat? Do they scream without a stop? Do they break down and sob uncontrollably?

Surely, I can't be the only one who feels morally obliged to publically confess, to be held accountable?

And yet most of the murderers remain unpunished.

When my cruel, wicked and unforgivable crimes were revealed to me, I knew immediately what I needed to do. I had no alternative.

I want you to know that I consulted with a psychiatrist for a number of months to help me confront this horrific unfolding

A World of Pains, Solly Kaplinski, 2015

nightmare. I am so grateful to him for his unconditional support and for liberating me from my pain and suffering. You may one day want to meet and thank Doctor Max Bromberg, but please, I beg you, I implore you, don't be angry with him. He is not too blame for the final and inevitable decision I made.

The responsibility is mine – and mine alone.

Sandrineleh, my beloved, my beauty, I have cherished and loved you so much – more than you will ever know. My biggest regret is that I could not share this burden with you and our sons. I had no words … and like me, I am sure that you have no words today. You are stunned, shocked, hurt and deeply wounded….and humiliated.

As much as I wanted to I couldn't talk with you about my ugly past, about my shame, about my innermost fears and anxieties, about the murderous part of me which was buried and hidden for so many years and exploded almost without warning back into my life.

Please, please forgive me for not confiding in you, for not telling you the truth about me. I am so sorry. I couldn't bring myself to do it. I was a coward. I simply never had the courage. And if I couldn't face myself, how in heaven's name could I face you?

I also wanted so much to protect you - hoping for the best outcome: that I was just a bystander, but fearing for the worst - that I was a brutal murderer. I think I also wanted to protect myself and my good name - and my dignity.

This may sound selfish but what was always important for me is that you, who I have admired and have put on a pedestal, should hold me in high esteem, that you should respect me and that I should not let you down. But all is lost. I failed you, our wonderful sons - and myself so miserably. Ruben and David, I worry so much for them now and how they will cope. My hurt and scarred darling, my wounded love, there are tears in my heart and on this page. I miss you so much and ache for you. I want so desperately to be with you now, to hold and comfort you, to feel the touch of your hand and the warmth of your kiss.

I can't ask you to mourn for me, to grieve for me and to cry for me. Leave my gravesite unmarked, with no tombstone and no inscription. I don't even deserve a *Kaddish* to be said for me.

Perhaps one day my love, with the passage of time, when I am hopefully a distant and faded memory and you have somehow found a way to move on from this awful tragedy, think only this of me:

A World of Pains, Solly Kaplinski, 2015

Perhaps his life had some meaning, that for a time, he was an upright person of integrity with the crown of a good name, that he was destined to accomplish something worthwhile, and that despite the horrors of his evil deeds, he achieved just a little good."

The Varnas home: December 16, 1996

"Mrs. Varnas, we have never met. I am Doctor Max Bromberg. Jonathan was in therapy with me for several months. I am deeply sorry for your tragic loss and I am so upset to meet you in this heartbreaking situation. I can't begin to imagine the grief and pain and hurt you are feeling."

Sandra is pale and gaunt. It is clear to Max that she is still in shock. Her eyes are glazed over. She barely registers and doesn't say a word. Her handshake is limp. She is unable to stand unaided. Ruben and David are holding her up.

Max points to a chair. They sit her down slowly. He sits opposite her.

"I want you to know that Jonathan loved you with all his heart, passionately and intensely, that you were the center of his universe. I know that it doesn't make it any easier for you but he wanted so much to share what he was going through with you but he was unable to do so. He simply couldn't bring himself to do it. He wanted to shield you …and himself."

Max is not sure if Sandra is taking in his words. There is no eye contact. He is aware that Ruben and David are glaring at him angrily. He knows that they resent his presence.

"One thing he said to me quoting a Navajo proverb" continues Max, "which I will never forget: 'You can't see the future with so many tears in your eyes.'

Mrs. Varnas, you don't know me at all but even though we are meeting for the first time, if you would like my support or help in any way, if you want to talk when you are ready, to unburden, to open your heart, I am here for you."

Max thinks he detects the veneer of a faint smile on her face. He imagines that she is saying to herself:

'That bastard! He's a miserable piece of shit. He wants to help me after he was responsible for my husband's death. May he rot in hell!'

There is a prolonged silence in the room. Those who have come to pay their respects stop talking.

Sandra's eyes are closed. Tears start running down her cheeks. She starts sobbing and tries to stifle her crying.

"Mrs. Varnas," says Max quietly, "please, please let yourself go. Don't bottle it up."

Sandra breaks down. She is keening hysterically and is unable to stop. Max reaches out to hold her cold hands gently but firmly.

The mournful lament continues.

Max stands up and puts his arm around her shoulders.

"Doctor Bromberg, I think you should leave now," says Ruben. "I want you to leave immediately. Your behavior is inappropriate...don't you dare touch my mother. Haven't you done enough damage to our family? Please go."

David stands up and looks at Max threateningly.

Max looks at Sandra. Her face is stooped. She is now keeled over in the chair, shoulders slouched, lifeless, her breathing is labored.

All eyes are fixed on Max. He looks at Sandra again. There is no response.

Max dejectedly makes his way to the front door.

In a barely audible voice, Sandra whispers,

"No! Wait. Dr. Bromberg, I...I need you to stay... I am wounded ... so broken and lost... What's going to happen to me, to *mein shayneh kinderlach*, my two beautiful boys? What's going to become of us? *Hoht rahmones* dear God, have mercy...."

Sandra tries vainly to wipe away her tears.

"Jonathan... Yonas....Kanas...mommy, oh mommy... my beloved *tateleh*... Doctor Bromberg, a part of me is missing ...I am broken and ... hurting and ...feel so empty inside. I...I want to know everything about Jonathan...but...but not today. I have no strength. I need you to ... to comfort me."

Sandra slowly and hesitatingly stands up, unaided. She is a little unsteady on her feet. Max puts his arms around Sandra and hugs her. She feels safe and secure and doesn't let go.

A World of Pains, Solly Kaplinski, 2015

Epilogue

Any Case

It could have happened.
It had to happen.
It happened earlier. Later.
Closer. Farther away.
It happened, but not to you.

You survived because you were first.
You survived because you were last.
Because alone. Because the others.
Because on the left. Because on the right.
Because it was raining. Because it was sunny.
Because a shadow fell.

Luckily there was a forest.
Luckily there were no trees.
Luckily a rail, a hook, a beam, a brake,
A frame, a turn, an inch, a second.
Luckily a straw was floating on the water.

Thanks to, thus, in spite of, and yet.

What would have happened if a hand, a leg,
One step, a hair away?

So you are here? Straight from that moment still suspended?
The net's mesh was tight, but you? through the mesh?
I can't stop wondering at it, can't be silent enough.
Listen,
How quickly your heart is beating in me.

Wislawa Szymborska

All Works by Wisława Szymborska © The Wisława Szymborska Foundation, **www.szymborska.org.pl**

Translated from the Polish by Grazyna Drabik and Sharon Olds
Reprinted by permission of Grazyna Drabik and Sharon Olds

Acknowledgements

I am deeply indebted to the following people who helped shepherd the process to shape and refine my thinking and ideas at various stages during this challenging journey. They have held my hand, stroked my ego and tried to discipline a stubborn first time novelist.

They are however not to blame for the shortcomings of the final product.

Arleen Leon Kaplinski: my life partner who accompanied me throughout this internal expedition and on our path together for the last 45 years.

Stephen D. Smith PhD: Andrew J. and Erna Finci Viterbi Executive Director Chair, USC Shoah Foundation for his invaluable and insightful ideas and suggestions and who captured the essence of the narrative in his very meaningful foreword. His excellent framing of the issues sets the tone for the novel.

Fania Brantsovsky: partisan during World War Two and librarian of the Vilnius Yiddish Institute. To walk with Fania in the Ponar forest in the snow is to relive its horrors but also to honor the memory of the victims and my grandparents in particular. One can't help but admire and be in awe of Fania's drive and tenacity, her determination to tell the story and her stubborn resistance in the face of the Lithuanian justice system who have targeted her as a war criminal! Now in her ninth decade – may she live until 120 (!), those who are privileged to spend time with Fania are changed forever.

Dovid Katz: former Professor of Yiddish Language, Literature and Culture at Vilnius University, Lithuania who helped ensure the veracity of the historical information in the text. Dovid is the bravest and most courageous person I know taking on virtually singlehandedly the Lithuanian authorities and the neo Nazis in Lithuania who are determined to revise and deny our tragic history. See his website:

www.defendinghistory.com

Robert Rozett: Director of Yad Vashem Libraries who assisted with historical information.

Wolfie Ze'ev Mankowitz, z"l *: my mentor for many years and at pivotal points of my career.

Lew Pullmer who helped sharpen the psychiatric/ psychological aspects of the narrative.

Tuvia Zabow for his insights and psychiatric expertise.

Hinrich Kaasmann: whose remarkable gesture of reconciliation between Germans and Jews demonstrated the transformative impact of an authentic apology.

Taffy Sassoon, Brenda Eisenberg, Joe Hoffman, Eddie Abramson and **Ronnie Gotkin** for their invaluable advice to make the story more readable. They tried!

Morris Wyszogrod, z"l* survivor, artist, and witness - for his translations of key documents and especially for teaching us that despite being trapped by the trauma of the Shoah and emphasizing time and again how important it is to remember – zachor (!), one could also lead parallel lives and move on to become a productive human being.

Ronit Kaplinski Mayer for her powerful cover illustration and for her editing expertise.

Julian Leon - an excellent sounding board virtually throughout the process. Also helped with research and keeping me on task!

*May his memory be for a blessing

References

Books

Arad, Y. (2012) The Holocaust in Lithuania and its obfuscation in Lithuanian sources
Retrieved from: **http://www.defendinghistory.com**

Balberyszski, M. (2010) Stronger than Iron: The Destruction of Vilna Jewry 1941 – 1945. Gefen Jerusalem

Browning, C. (1993) Ordinary Men: Reserve Police Battalion 101 and the Final Solution in Poland. Harper Perennial

Kaplinski, S. (1992) Lost and Found – A Second Generation Response to the Holocaust. Creda Press

Kaplinski, S. (2008) Flickering Margins. Unpublished manuscript 2008

Melamed, J. A. (1999) Lithuania – Crime and Punishment Periodical

Nuremberg, E. B (1936) *Trau keinem Fuchs auf grüner Heid und keinem Jud auf seinem Eid. Trust No Fox on his Green Heath and No Jew on his Oath.* Stürmer Verlag

Rhodes, R. (2002) Masters of Death - The SS- Einsatzgruppen and the invention of the Holocaust. Alfred A Knopf New York

Rozett, R. and Spector, S.   (2009) Encyclopedia of the Holocaust.
Lambda Publishers Inc.

Sakowicz , K. (2005) Ponary Diary 1941 – 1943
A bystander's account of a mass murder. Yale University Press

Urich, A. The Nazi Death Machine: Hitler's Drugged Soldiers
Translated from the German by Sultan, C. 2005

Newspaper Articles

The Last News. Yiddish newspaper (published in Israel 1949 – 2006)

Retribution: Cape Town Man to give evidence against his Nazi tormentors
Dennis Herbstein, Cape Times Weekend Magazine May 29 1965

Cape Town doctor to testify against S.S. massacre men
Sunday Times correspondent, South African Sunday Times May 18 1969

How therapists mourn
Robin Weiss: New York Times, July 4, 2015

Document

The Public Prosecutor's Office of the Mainz District Court:
Prosecution of Windisch et.al for Murder: Preliminary
proceedings: Evidence of Dr. I Kaplinski June 15 1965

Other Sources
Tillman, J. G. (2014) Patient Suicide: Impact on Clinicians,
Retrieved from Psychiatric Times, December 31, 2014

http://www.psychiatrictimes.com/special-reports/patient-
suicide-impact-clinicians#sthash.8HjYVq94.dpuf

Recovered Memory Therapy
Retrieved from:

http://www.betterhealth.vic.gov.au/bhcv2/bhcarticles.nsf/pa
ges/Recovered_memory_therapy

Dream Interpretation

Retrieved from:

http://dreaminterpretation8.blogspot.co.il/2008/01/what-
dreams-about-eyes-mean.html

The Reality of Repressed Memories

Retrieved from:

http://faculty.washington.edu/eloftus/Articles/lof93.htm

The Jews are our misfortune

Retrieved from:

http://germanhistorydocs.ghi-
dc.org/sub_document.cfm?document_id=1799

Declaration of 75 Notables against Antisemitism

Retrieved from:

http://germanhistorydocs.ghi-
dc.org/sub_document.cfm?document_id=1803

IAF Jets over Auschwitz

Retrieved from:

http://www.idf.il/1283-15677-en/Dover.aspx

The Extermination of the Jews in Ivye

Retrieved from:

http://www.jewishgen.org/yizkor/ivye/ivy503.html

Testimony of Dr. Izak Kaplinski

Retrieved from:

http://kehilalinks.jewishgen.org/lida-district/kaplinski.htm

The Nizkor Project - Propaganda and Children during the Hitler Years

Retrieved from:

http://www.nizkor.org/hweb/people/m/mills-mary/mills-00.html

Navajo proverb

Retrieved from:

http://www.walnutridgeconsulting.com/?page_id=376

Yad Vashem

Retrieved from:

http://www.yadvashem.org/

Song

Complete me

Words and Music: Solly Kaplinski

Unpublished circa 1980's

Author's Biography

Solly Kaplinski lives and works in Jerusalem.

His late parents, of blessed memory, were Holocaust survivors who came to South Africa in 1947. They spent several years with the Bielski partisans in the Nalibocka forest in Western Belarus engaged in rescue, resistance and sabotage missions.

An alumnus of Herzlia School in Cape Town, the Habonim Zionist youth movement and of the Universities of Cape Town and South Africa, Solly commenced his professional career in education as a school guidance counselor and clinical psychologist.

He was the Headmaster of Jewish Community Day Schools in South Africa and Canada before immigrating to Israel with his wife, Arleen, in 2000.

Formerly the Director of the International Relations English Desk at Yad Vashem, he is currently engaged as Executive Director, Overseas Joint Ventures, at the American Jewish Joint Distribution Committee.

A World of Pains, Solly Kaplinski, 2015

A graduate of the Jerusalem Fellows Program and of the Harvard University Principals' Center, Solly is also a published poet and author. His poetry has appeared in several university anthologies.

Solly is especially moved by and takes pride in the fact that the Kaplinski family – three children and nine grandchildren, has regenerated itself after the rupture of the Shoah and has taken root and is flourishing in Israel.

Finale

The trees of Ponar: A failed blood transfusion

Ballet has a new meaning for me now:

the trees of Ponar

somehow remind me of

ballet dancers

so elegant and graceful

in repose

Just think:

as saplings they were suckled

not on mother's milk,

the stuff of human kindness

but on the

blood of my brothers

scattered all over

this accepting earth.

Pity these selfsame trees can't bear witness to

their experience

as saplings.

The young somehow always have

a clearer vision.

Solly Kaplinski, 1992

A World of Pains, Solly Kaplinski, 2015

Made in the USA
Middletown, DE
06 April 2016